PRO...
FOR LIFE

=== ❧ ===

is a

Special Gift to

_____

(name)

on

_____

(date)

by

_____

(name)

PROMISES FOR LIFE

Bible Passages
for Comfort, Encouragement, and Guidance

from

The Promise™
Contemporary English Version

Thomas Nelson Publishers
Nashville • Atlanta • London • Vancouver

1 2 3 4 5 6 7 8 9 — 99 98 97 96 95

Introduction

🙿 Centuries before the Bible was completed, the psalmist wrote at Psalm 119.105,

> Your word is a lamp that gives light wherever I walk.

That same regard for the Word of God continues to be shared by millions who experience the sin and confusion of today. The Word of God is for all people a light by which to walk through the darkness of this world.

Someone has said that there are more than thirty-seven thousand promises in the Word of God. *Promises For Life* makes the most prominent of those readily available in a systematic form. The themes covered relate to the most vital needs of everyday living.

The book is designed for use in personal devotions. It can also be effective when used by pastors and other Christian workers in counseling, hospital and shut-in visitation, and in other situations where one requires Bible passages in a topical arrangement.

Welcome to the Contemporary English Version

Languages are spoken before they are written. And far more communication is done through the spoken word than through the written word. In fact, more people *hear* the Bible read than read it for themselves. Traditional translations of the Bible count on the *reader's* ability to understand a *written* text. But the *Contemporary English Version* differs from all other English Bibles—past and present—in that it takes into consideration the needs of the *hearer,* as well as those of the reader, who may not be familiar with traditional biblical language.

The *Contemporary English Version* has been described as a "user-friendly" and a "mission-driven" translation that can be *read aloud* without stumbling, *heard* without misunderstanding, and *listened to* with enjoyment and appreciation, because the language is contemporary and the style is lucid and lyrical.

The *Contemporary English Version* invites you to *read,* to *understand* and to *share*
the Word of God now
as never before!

Contents

Your thoughts are far beyond
my understanding,
    much more than I could
    ever imagine. PSALM 139.17

The Bible— Our Source Book

🕬 Everything in the Scriptures is God's Word. All of it is useful for teaching and helping people and for correcting them and showing them how to live. The Scriptures train God's servants to do all kinds of good deeds.   2 TIMOTHY 3.16–17

What God has said isn't only alive and active! It is sharper than any double-edged sword. His word can cut through our spirits and souls and through our joints and marrow, until it discovers the desires and thoughts of our hearts.   HEBREWS 4.12

Anyone who hears and obeys these teachings of mine is like a wise person who built a house on solid rock. Rain poured down, rivers flooded, and winds beat against that house. But it did not fall, because it was built on solid rock.

MATTHEW 7.24–25

1

Knowing these teachings
   will mean true life
   and good health for you.

PROVERBS 4.22

The sky and the earth will not last
forever, but my words will.   MARK 13.31

The LORD made the heavens
   and everything in them by his word.

PSALM 33.6

Everyone in this world should worship
   and honor the LORD!
As soon as he spoke the world was created;
   at his command, the earth was formed.

PSALM 33.8-9

I tell you for certain that everyone who
hears my message and has faith in the one
who sent me has eternal life and will never
be condemned. They have already gone
from death to life.   JOHN 5.24

Praise the LORD! He has kept his promise
and given us peace. Every good thing he
promised to his servant Moses has
happened.   I KINGS 8.56

The Bible—
Our Comfort

When I am hurting,
  I find comfort in your promise
  that leads to life.   PSALM 119.50

The Law of the LORD is perfect;
it gives us new life.
His teachings last forever,
  and they give wisdom
  to ordinary people.
The LORD's instruction is right;
  it makes our hearts glad.
His commands shine brightly,
and they give us light.   PSALM 19.7–8

Everything God says is true—
  and it's a shield for all
  who come to him for safety.

                              PROVERBS 30.5

My child, remember
my teachings and instructions
  and obey them completely.

3

They will help you live
a long and prosperous life.

PROVERBS 3.1-2

You give peace of mind
to all who love your Law.
    Nothing can make them fall.

PSALM 119.165

There are many rooms in my Father's
house. I wouldn't tell you this, unless it was
true. I am going there to prepare a place for
each of you. After I have done this, I will
come back and take you with me. Then we
will be together. You know the way to where
I am going.   JOHN 14.2-4

God is our mighty fortress,
    always ready to help in times of trouble.

PSALM 46.1

So if you belong to Christ, you are now
part of Abraham's family, and you will be
given what God has promised.

GALATIANS 3.29

I won't ever forget your teachings,
    because you give me new life
    by following them.   PSALM 119.93

The Bible—Our Guide

❧ If any of you need wisdom, you should
ask God, and it will be given to you.

JAMES 1.5

The Law of the Lord is a lamp,
    and its teachings shine brightly.

PROVERBS 6.23

If you do what the LORD wants,
    he will make certain
    each step you take is sure.
The LORD will hold your hand,
    and if you stumble, you still won't fall.

PSALM 37.23–24

But now you will again see the Lord,
your teacher, and he will guide you. Whether
you turn to the right or to the left, you will

hear a voice saying, "This is the road! Now
follow it." ISAIAH 30.20-21

With all your heart you must trust the LORD
  and not your own judgment.
Always let him lead you,
  and he will clear the road
  for you to follow. PROVERBS 3.5-6

You, LORD God, are my mighty rock
and my fortress.
Lead me and guide me,
  so that your name will be honored.

PSALM 31.3

But I never really left you,
and you hold my right hand.
Your advice has been my guide,
  and later you will welcome me in glory.

PSALM 73.23-24

Jesus told the people who had faith in
him, "If you keep on obeying what I have
said, you truly are my disciples. You will
know the truth, and the truth will set you
free." JOHN 8.31-32

Our LORD and God, you are my lamp.
You turn darkness to light.

2 SAMUEL 22.29

You said to me, "I will point out the road
    that you should follow.
I will be your teacher and watch over you."

PSALM 32.8

The Bible—Our Strength

❧ But those who trust the LORD
will find new strength.
They will be strong like eagles
soaring upward on wings;
    they will walk and run
    without getting tired.   ISAIAH 40.31

I now place you in God's care.
Remember the message about his great
kindness! This message can help you and
give you what belongs to you as God's
people.   ACTS 20.32

7

Your way is perfect, LORD,
and your word is correct.
    You are a shield for those
    who run to you for help.   PSALM 18.30

    Do this because God has given you new
birth by his message that lives on forever.
                    1 PETER 1.23

But what the LORD has planned
will stand forever.
    His thoughts never change.
                    PSALM 33.11

    Praise the LORD! He has kept his promise
and given us peace. Every good thing he
promised to his servant Moses has
happened.   1 KINGS 8.56

I am overcome with sorrow.
    Encourage me,
    as you have promised to do.
                    PSALM 119.28

God is always honest and fair,
and his laws can be trusted.
    They are true and right
    and will stand forever.   PSALM 111.7-8

The Need for God's Help

🕊 Jesus replied, "I tell you for certain that you must be born from above before you can see God's kingdom!"   JOHN 3.3

Sin pays off with death. But God's gift is eternal life given by Jesus Christ our Lord.
ROMANS 6.23

But you are stubborn and refuse to turn to God. So you are making things even worse for yourselves on that day when he will show how angry he is and will judge the world with fairness.   ROMANS 2.5

Don't let anyone trick you with foolish talk. God punishes everyone who disobeys him and says foolish things.
EPHESIANS 5.6

If our minds are ruled by our desires, we will die. But if our minds are ruled by the Spirit, we will have life and peace. Our desires fight against God, because they do not and cannot obey God's laws. If we follow our desires, we cannot please God.

ROMANS 8.6-8

All of us have sinned and fallen short of God's glory.   ROMANS 3.23

What a miserable person I am. Who will rescue me from this body that is doomed to die? Thank God! Jesus Christ will rescue me.   ROMANS 7.24-25

The Lord isn't slow about keeping his promises, as some people think he is. In fact, God is patient, because he wants everyone to turn from sin and no one to be lost.   2 PETER 3.9

God's Desire to Help

❧ The Son of Man came to look for and to save people who are lost.   LUKE 19.10

God loved the people of this world so much that he gave his only Son, so that everyone who has faith in him will have eternal life and never really die.

JOHN 3.16

The Scriptures say, "God commanded light to shine in the dark." Now God is shining in our hearts to let you know that his glory is seen in Jesus Christ.

2 CORINTHIANS 4.6

God did not send his Son into the world to condemn its people. He sent him to save them! JOHN 3.17

I told you the most important part of the message exactly as it was told to me. That part is:
Christ died for our sins,
as the Scriptures say.

1 CORINTHIANS 15.3

Then after her baby is born, name him Jesus, because he will save his people from their sins. MATTHEW 1.21

Christ sacrificed his life's blood to set us free, which means that our sins are now forgiven. EPHESIANS 1.7

But God treats us much better than we deserve, and because of Christ Jesus, he freely accepts us and sets us free from our sins.   ROMANS 3.24

Even when we were God's enemies, he made peace with us, because his Son died for us. Yet something even greater than friendship is ours. Now that we are at peace with God, we will be saved by his Son's life.

ROMANS 5.10

Christ died for us at a time when we were helpless and sinful. No one is really willing to die for an honest person, though someone might be willing to die for a truly good person. But God showed how much he loved us by having Christ die for us, even though we were sinful.   ROMANS 5.6-8

The Freely Given Love of God

❧ You were saved by faith in God, who treats us much better than we deserve. This

is God's gift to you, and not anything you
have done on your own.   EPHESIANS 2.8

God saved us and chose us
to be his holy people.
We did nothing to deserve this,
    but God planned it
    because he is so kind.
Even before time began
    God planned for Christ Jesus
    to show kindness to us.

2 TIMOTHY 1.9

But the gift that God was kind enough
to give was very different from Adam's sin.
That one sin brought death to many others.
Yet in an even greater way, Jesus Christ
alone brought God's gift of kindness to
many people.   ROMANS 5.15

Then I will take away your stubbornness
and make you eager to be completely
faithful to me. You will want to obey me and
all my laws and teachings. You will be my
people, and I will be your God.

EZEKIEL 11.19–20

Our LORD and our God, you are like the sun
    and also like a shield.
You treat us with kindness and with honor,
    never denying any good thing
    to those who live right.   PSALM 84.11

    So whenever we are in need, we should
come bravely before the throne of our
merciful God. There we will be treated with
undeserved kindness, and we will find help.
                                        HEBREWS 4.16

Firm Belief

❧ I know about my sins,
    and I cannot forget my terrible guilt.
You are really the one I have sinned against;
    I have disobeyed you
    and have done wrong.
So it is right and fair for you
    to correct and punish me.
                            PSALM 51.3-4

The way to please you
    is to feel sorrow deep in our hearts.

14

This is the kind of sacrifice
you won't refuse.   PSALM 51.17

    The jailer asked for a torch and went
into the jail. He was shaking all over as he
knelt down in front of Paul and Silas. After
he had led them out of the jail, he asked,
"What must I do to be saved?"

ACTS 16.29–30

    Then I cried out, "I'm doomed!
Everything I say is sinful, and so are the
words of everyone around me. Yet I have
seen the King, the LORD All-Powerful."

ISAIAH 6.5

Won't you look and see
how upset I am, our LORD?
My stomach is in knots,
and my heart is broken
    because I betrayed you.

LAMENTATIONS 1.20

Then speak, and I will reply;
    or else let me speak, and you reply.
Please point out my sins,
so I will know them.   JOB 13.22–23

Faith

🕊 But Jesus told the woman, "Because of your faith, you are now saved. May God give you peace!" LUKE 7.50

Then he said to Jesus, "Remember me when you come into power!"

Jesus replied, "I promise that today you will be with me in paradise."

LUKE 23.42–43

This message made the Gentiles glad, and they praised what they had heard about the Lord. Everyone who had been chosen for eternal life then put their faith in the Lord.

ACTS 13.48

A woman who had been bleeding for twelve years came up behind Jesus and barely touched his clothes. She had said to herself, "If I can just touch his clothes, I will get well."

Jesus turned. He saw the woman and said, "Don't worry! You are now well because of your faith." At that moment she was healed. MATTHEW 9.20–22

No one can have faith without hearing the message about Christ.   ROMANS 10.17

Anyone who believes me and is baptized will be saved. But anyone who refuses to believe me will be condemned.

MARK 16.16

But the officer said, "Lord, I'm not good enough for you to come into my house. Just give the order, and my servant will get well. I have officers who give orders to me, and I have soldiers who take orders from me. I can say to one of them, 'Go!' and he goes. I can say to another, 'Come!' and he comes. I can say to my servant, 'Do this!' and he will do it."

When Jesus heard this, he was so surprised that he turned and said to the crowd following him, "I tell you that in all of Israel I've never found anyone with this much faith!"   MATTHEW 8.8-10

But without faith no one can please God. We must believe that God is real and that he rewards everyone who searches for him.

HEBREWS 11.6

You were saved by faith in God, who treats us much better than we deserve. This is God's gift to you, and not anything you have done on your own.   EPHESIANS 2.8

Jesus then said, "I am the one who raises the dead to life! Everyone who has faith in me will live, even if they die. And everyone who lives because of faith in me will never really die."   JOHN 11.25–26

Turning Back to God

🕮 I didn't come to invite good people to turn to God. I came to invite sinners.

LUKE 5.32

Then the Lord will save everyone
    who asks for his help.   ACTS 2.21

If you really want to live,
you must stop doing wrong
    and start doing right.
I, the LORD God All-Powerful,
will then be on your side,
    just as you claim I am.   AMOS 5.14

18

The LORD told me to stand by the gate of the temple and to tell the people who were going in that the LORD All-Powerful, the God of Israel, had said:

Pay attention, people of Judah! Change your ways and start living right, then I will let you keep on living in your own country. Don't fool yourselves! My temple is here in Jerusalem, but that doesn't mean I will protect you. I will keep you safe only if you change your ways. Be fair and honest with each other. Stop taking advantage of foreigners, orphans, and widows. Don't kill innocent people. And stop worshiping other gods. Then I will let you enjoy a long life in this land I gave your ancestors.

JEREMIAH 7.1–7

Years later, John the Baptist started preaching in the desert of Judea. He said, "Turn back to God! The kingdom of heaven will soon be here." MATTHEW 3.1–2

Peter said, "Turn back to God! Be baptized in the name of Jesus Christ, so that your sins will be forgiven. Then you will

19

be given the Holy Spirit. This promise is for you and your children. It is for everyone our Lord God will choose, no matter where they live." ACTS 2.38-39

The Lord isn't slow about keeping his promises, as some people think he is. In fact, God is patient, because he wants everyone to turn from sin and no one to be lost. 2 PETER 3.9

Surrender to God! Resist the devil, and he will run from you. Come near to God, and he will come near to you. Clean up your lives, you sinners. JAMES 4.7-8

If we say that we have not sinned, we are fooling ourselves, and the truth isn't in our hearts. But if we confess our sins to God, he can always be trusted to forgive us and take our sins away. 1 JOHN 1.8-9

Don't you know that the reason God is good to you is because he wants you to turn to him? ROMANS 2.4

Confession

❧ From all Judea and Jerusalem crowds of people went to John. They told how sorry they were for their sins, and he baptized them in the Jordan River. MARK 1.5

So I confessed my sins
and told them all to you.
    I said, "I'll tell the LORD
    each one of my sins."
Then you forgave me
and took away my guilt. PSALM 32.5

So you will be saved, if you honestly say, "Jesus is Lord," and if you believe with all your heart that God raised him from death. God will accept you and save you, if you truly believe this and tell it to others.

ROMANS 10.9–10

If you tell others that you belong to me, I will tell my Father in heaven that you are my followers. MATTHEW 10.32

If you have sinned, you should tell each other what you have done. Then you can pray for one another and be healed. The prayer of an innocent person is powerful, and it can help a lot. JAMES 5.16

If we say that we have not sinned, we are fooling ourselves, and the truth isn't in our hearts. But if we confess our sins to God, he can always be trusted to forgive us and take our sins away. 1 JOHN 1.8–9

And to the glory of God the Father
everyone will openly agree,
    "Jesus Christ is Lord!"

PHILIPPIANS 2.11

Acceptance

❧ All who call out to the Lord will be saved. ROMANS 10.13

With all my heart I praise the LORD,
    and with all that I am
    I praise his holy name!
With all my heart I praise the LORD!
    I will never forget how kind he has been.

The LORD forgives our sins,
heals us when we are sick,
   and protects us from death.
His kindness and love
are a crown on our heads.
Each day that we live,
he provides for our needs
   and gives us the strength
   of a young eagle. PSALM 103.1–5

Our God, no one is like you.
We are all that is left of your chosen people,
   and you freely forgive our sin and guilt.
You don't stay angry forever;
you're glad to have pity
   and pleased to be merciful.
You will trample on our sins
   and throw them in the sea.

           MICAH 7.18–19

   Christ never sinned! But God treated
him as a sinner, so that Christ could make
us acceptable to God. 2 CORINTHIANS 5.21

   "So I tell you that all her sins are
forgiven, and that is why she has shown
great love. But anyone who has been

forgiven for only a little will show only a little love."

Then Jesus said to the woman, "Your sins are forgiven." LUKE 7.47-48

We are careful not to judge people by what they seem to be, though we once judged Christ in that way. Anyone who belongs to Christ is a new person. The past is forgotten, and everything is new.
2 CORINTHIANS 5.16-17

On the cross Christ did away with our hatred for each other. He also made peace between us and God by uniting Jews and Gentiles in one body. Christ came and preached peace to you Gentiles, who were far from God, and peace to us Jews, who were near God. And because of Christ, all of us can come to the Father by the same Spirit. EPHESIANS 2.16-18

You used to be far from God. Your thoughts made you his enemies, and you did evil things. But his Son became a human and died. So God made peace with you, and now he lets you stand in his presence as people who are holy and

faultless and innocent. But you must stay
deeply rooted and firm in your faith. You
must not give up the hope you received
when you heard the good news. It was
preached to everyone on earth, and I myself
have become a servant of this message.

COLOSSIANS 1.21-23

Everything and everyone that the Father
has given me will come to me, and I won't
turn any of them away. JOHN 6.37

Everyone was going to be punished
because Adam sinned. But because of the
good thing that Christ has done, God
accepts us and gives us the gift of life.
Adam disobeyed God and caused many
others to be sinners. But Jesus obeyed him
and will make many people acceptable to
God. ROMANS 5.18-19

Being Acceptable to God

❧ But we know that God accepts only
those who have faith in Jesus Christ. No
one can please God by simply obeying the

Law. So we put our faith in Christ Jesus,
and God accepted us because of our faith.

GALATIANS 2.16

You were dead, because you were sinful
and were not God's people. But God let
Christ make you alive, when he forgave
all our sins.
God wiped out the charges that were
against us for disobeying the Law of Moses.
He took them away and nailed them to the
cross.   COLOSSIANS 2.13–14

The Law was our teacher. It was
supposed to teach us until we had faith and
were acceptable to God.   GALATIANS 3.24

Jesus treated us much better
than we deserved.
He made us acceptable to God
    and gave us the hope of eternal life.

TITUS 3.7

I will treat them with kindness,
    even though they are wicked.
I will forget their sins.   HEBREWS 8.12

"Then I will forget about their sins
  and no longer remember
  their evil deeds."
When sins are forgiven, there is no more
need to offer sacrifices.

My friends, the blood of Jesus gives us
courage to enter the most holy place by a
new way that leads to life! And this way
takes us through the curtain that is Christ
himself.   HEBREWS 10.17-20

Abram believed the LORD, and the LORD
was pleased with him.   GENESIS 15.6

I am proud of the good news! It is God's
powerful way of saving all people who have
faith, whether they are Jews or Gentiles. The
good news tells how God accepts everyone
who has faith, but only those who have
faith. It is just as the Scriptures say, "The
people God accepts because of their faith
will live."   ROMANS 1.16-17

Just as God says in the Scriptures,
  "Look! I am placing in Zion
    a stone to make people
    stumble and fall.

But those who have faith in that one
will never be disappointed."

ROMANS 9.33

We are happy all day because of you,
and your saving power
brings honor to us.
Your own glorious power makes us strong,
and because of your kindness,
our strength increases.

PSALM 89.16–17

That's also how it is with people.
The ones who stop doing evil and make
themselves pure will become special. Their
lives will be holy and pleasing to their
Master, and they will be able to do all kinds
of good deeds.

Run from temptations that capture
young people. Always do the right thing. Be
faithful, loving, and easy to get along with.
Worship with people whose hearts are pure.

2 TIMOTHY 2.21–22

Our ancestor Abraham pleased God
by putting his son Isaac on the altar to
sacrifice him. Now you see how Abraham's
faith and deeds worked together. He proved

that his faith was real by what he did. This is what the Scriptures mean by saying, "Abraham had faith in God, and God was pleased with him." That's how Abraham became God's friend.   JAMES 2.21–23

Rescue

🐦 You will know the truth, and the truth will set you free.   JOHN 8.32

Our LORD, you bless those who live right,
    and you shield them with your kindness.
                                        PSALM 5.12

But he replied, "My kindness is all you need. My power is strongest when you are weak." So if Christ keeps giving me his power, I will gladly brag about how weak I am.   2 CORINTHIANS 12.9

Trust the LORD! Be brave and strong
and trust the LORD.   PSALM 27.14

But God set you free when he sent his own Son to be like us sinners and to be a

sacrifice for our sin. God used Christ's body
to condemn sin. He did this, so that we
would do what the Law commands by
obeying the Spirit instead of our own
desires.   ROMANS 8.3-4

What a miserable person I am. Who will
rescue me from this body that is doomed to
die? Thank God! Jesus Christ will rescue
me.   ROMANS 7.24-25

"The Lord watches over
  everyone who obeys him,
  and he listens to their prayers.
    But he opposes everyone
    who does evil."
Can anyone really harm you for being
eager to do good deeds?   1 PETER 3.12-13

The LORD loves justice,
    and he won't ever desert
    his faithful people.
He always protects them.   PSALM 37.28

Children, you belong to God, and you
have defeated these enemies. God's Spirit is
in you and is more powerful than the one
that is in the world.   1 JOHN 4.4

I pray that God the Father and our Lord Jesus Christ will be kind to you and will bless you with peace! Christ obeyed God our Father and gave himself as a sacrifice for our sins to rescue us from this evil world. GALATIANS 1.3–4

But the Lord can be trusted to make you strong and protect you from harm.

2 THESSALONIANS 3.3

Becoming God's Children

❧ God was kind and decided that Christ would choose us to be God's own adopted children. EPHESIANS 1.5

Think how much the Father loves us. He loves us so much that he lets us be called his children, as we truly are. But since the people of this world did not know who Christ is, they don't know who we are. My dear friends, we are already God's children, though what we will be hasn't yet been seen. But we do know that when Christ returns, we will be like him, because we will see him as he truly is.   1 JOHN 3.1-2

But when the time was right, God sent his Son, and a woman gave birth to him. His Son obeyed the Law, so he could set us free from the Law, and we could become God's children. Now that we are his children, God has sent the Spirit of his Son into our hearts. And his Spirit tells us that God is our Father. You are no longer slaves. You are God's children, and you will be given what he has promised.

GALATIANS 4.4-7

All of you are God's children because of your faith in Christ Jesus.

GALATIANS 3.26

We know that God is always at work for the good of everyone who loves him. They are the ones God has chosen for his purpose, and he has always known who his chosen ones would be. He had decided to let them become like his own Son, so that his Son would be the first of many children.

ROMANS 8.28-29

"The Lord corrects the people he loves
and disciplines those
he calls his own."
Be patient when you are being
corrected! This is how God treats his
children. Don't all parents correct their
children? HEBREWS 12.6-7

Then I will welcome you and be your Father.
You will be my sons and my daughters,
as surely as I am God, the all-powerful.
2 CORINTHIANS 6.17-18

Yet some people accepted him
and put their faith in him.
So he gave them the right
to be the children of God. JOHN 1.12

Standing Strong

🐛 Jesus said, "Simon, listen to me! Satan
has demanded the right to test each one of
you, as a farmer does when he separates
wheat from the husks. But Simon, I have
prayed that your faith will be strong. And
when you have come back to me, help the
others." LUKE 22.31-32

The LORD gives strength
to those who are weary.   ISAIAH 40.29

Here is a message for all who are weak,
	trembling, and worried:
"Cheer up! Don't be afraid.
	Your God is coming
	to punish your enemies.
God will take revenge on them
and rescue you."   ISAIAH 35.3-4

Everyone who wins the victory will wear
white clothes. Their names will not be
erased from the book of life, and I will tell
my Father and his angels that they are my
followers.   REVELATION 3.5

I'll strengthen my people
because of who I am,
and they will follow me.   ZECHARIAH 10.12

All who trust the LORD,
be cheerful and strong.   PSALM 31.24

We wish that each of you would always
be eager to show how strong and lasting
your hope really is. Then you would never be

lazy. You would be following the example of
those who had faith and were patient until
God kept his promise to them.

HEBREWS 6.11-12

Guidance

❧ I will lead the blind
on roads they have never known;
 I will guide them
 on paths they have never traveled.
Their road is dark and rough,
but I will give light
 to keep them from stumbling.
This is my solemn promise. ISAIAH 42.16

Then you can say to future generations,
"Our God is like this forever
and will always guide us." PSALM 48.13-14

With all your heart you must trust the LORD
 and not your own judgment.
Always let him lead you,
 and he will clear the road
 for you to follow. PROVERBS 3.5-6

We make our own plans,
   but the LORD decides where we will go.
PROVERBS 16.9

But I never really left you,
and you hold my right hand.
Your advice has been my guide,
   and later you will welcome me in glory.
PSALM 73.23-24

And at this very moment,
God deeply desires to lead you from trouble
   and to spread your table
   with your favorite food.   JOB 36.16

The Spirit shows what is true and will
come and guide you into the full truth.
JOHN 16.13

Faith and Trust

❧ No one can have faith without hearing the message about Christ.   ROMANS 10.17

I realize how kind God has been to me, and so I tell each of you not to think you are better than you really are. Use good sense and measure yourself by the amount of faith that God has given you.

ROMANS 12.3

The LORD is constantly watching everyone, and he gives strength to those who faithfully obey him.

2 CHRONICLES 16.9

Your faith will be like gold that has been tested in a fire. And these trials will prove that your faith is worth much more than gold that can be destroyed. They will show that you will be given praise and honor and glory when Jesus Christ returns.

You have never seen Jesus, and you don't see him now. But still you love him and have faith in him, and no words can tell how glad and happy you are to be saved. That's why you have faith. 1 PETER 1.7-9

But the Lord can be trusted to make you strong and protect you from harm.
2 THESSALONIANS 3.3

But without faith no one can please God. We must believe that God is real and that he rewards everyone who searches for him.
HEBREWS 11.6

Faith makes us sure of what we hope for and gives us proof of what we cannot see.
HEBREWS 11.1

Love for God

❧ You know that the LORD your God is the only true God. So love him and obey his commands, and he will faithfully keep his agreement with you and your descendants for a thousand generations.
DEUTERONOMY 7.9

But it is just as the Scriptures say,
"What God has planned
for people who love him
is more than eyes have seen
or ears have heard.
It has never even
entered our minds!"

1 CORINTHIANS 2.9

Jesus answered, "The most important one says: 'People of Israel, you have only one Lord and God. You must love him with all your heart, soul, mind, and strength.'"

MARK 12.29-30

God will bless you, if you don't give up when your faith is being tested. He will reward you with a glorious life, just as he rewards everyone who loves him.

JAMES 1.12

Real love isn't our love for God, but his love for us. God sent his Son to be the sacrifice by which our sins are forgiven. Dear friends, since God loved us this much, we must love each other. 1 JOHN 4.10-11

If you love me, you will do what I have said, and my Father will love you. I will also love you and show you what I am like.

JOHN 14.21

God the Father loves you because you love me, and you believe that I have come from him.   JOHN 16.27

Love for Others

❧ But if we love others, we are in the light, and we don't cause problems for them. If we hate others, we are living and walking in the dark. We don't know where we are going, because we can't see in the dark.   1 JOHN 2.10-11

But I tell you to love your enemies and pray for anyone who mistreats you.

MATTHEW 5.44

The second most important commandment says: "Love others as much as you love yourself."

MARK 12.31

Dear friends don't try to get even. Let
God take revenge. In the Scriptures the
Lord says,
>"I am the one to take revenge
>and pay them back."

The Scriptures also say,
>"If your enemies are hungry,
>give them something to eat.
>And if they are thirsty,
>give them something to drink.
>This will be the same
>as piling burning coals
>on their heads."

Don't let evil defeat you, but defeat evil with
good.   ROMANS 12.19–21

What if I could speak
all languages of humans
   and of angels?
If I did not love others,
I would be nothing more than a noisy gong
   or a clanging cymbal.
What if I could prophesy
   and understand all secrets
   and all knowledge?
And what if I had faith
that moved mountains?
   I would be nothing, unless I loved others.

41

What if I gave away all that I owned
and let myself be burned alive?
    I would gain nothing,
    unless I loved others.
Love is kind and patient,
    never jealous, boastful,
    proud, or rude.
Love isn't selfish or quick tempered.
    It doesn't keep a record
    of wrongs that others do.
Love rejoices in the truth, but not in evil.
Love is always supportive,
loyal, hopeful, and trusting.
    Love never fails! 1 CORINTHIANS 13.1-8

But don't forget to help others and to
share your possessions with them. This too
is like offering a sacrifice that pleases God.
HEBREWS 13.16

God is always fair. He will remember
how you helped his people in the past and
how you are still helping them. You belong
to God, and he won't forget the love you
have shown his people. HEBREWS 6.10

Now I tell you to love each other, as I have loved you. The greatest way to show love for friends is to die for them.

JOHN 15.12–13

But if we love each other, God lives in us, and his love is truly in our hearts.

1 JOHN 4.12

Peace

I will listen to you, Lord God, because you promise peace to those
   who are faithful and no longer foolish.

PSALM 85.8

I pray that God, who gives hope, will bless you with complete happiness and peace because of your faith. And may the power of the Holy Spirit fill you with hope.

ROMANS 15.13

God's kingdom isn't about eating and drinking. It is about pleasing God, about living in peace, and about true happiness. All this comes from the Holy Spirit. If you serve Christ in this way, you will please God and be respected by people. We should try to live at peace and help each other have a strong faith. ROMANS 14.17–19

I pray that the Lord, who gives peace, will always bless you with peace. May the Lord be with all of you.

2 THESSALONIANS 3.16

Good-by, my friends. Do better and pay attention to what I have said. Try to get along and live peacefully with each other.

2 CORINTHIANS 13.11

Think of the bright future waiting
for all the families of honest
    and innocent and peace-loving people.

PSALM 37.37

I give you peace, the kind of peace that only I can give. It isn't like the peace that this world can give. So don't be worried or afraid. JOHN 14.27

44

Don't worry about anything, but pray about everything. With thankful hearts offer up your prayers and requests to God. Then, because you belong to Christ Jesus, God will bless you with peace that no one can completely understand. And this peace will control the way you think and feel.

PHILIPPIANS 4.6–7

Maturity

God is the one who began this good work in you, and I am certain that he won't stop before it is complete on the day that Christ Jesus returns.   PHILIPPIANS 1.6

Search for wisdom
    as you would search for silver
    or hidden treasure.
Then you will understand
what it means to respect
    and to know the LORD God.

All wisdom comes from the LORD,
    and so do common sense
    and understanding.

45

God gives helpful advice
to everyone who obeys him
    and protects all of those
    who live as they should.

PROVERBS 2.4–7

You said to me, "I will point out the road
    that you should follow.
I will be your teacher and watch over you."

PSALM 32.8

Respect and obey the LORD!
This is the first step
to wisdom and good sense.

PSALM 111.10

Let the wonderful kindness and the
understanding that come from our Lord
and Savior Jesus Christ help you to keep
on growing. Praise Jesus now and
forever! Amen. 2 PETER 3.18

If any of you need wisdom, you should
ask God, and it will be given to you.

JAMES 1.5

46

Forgiving Others

❧ Peter came up to the Lord and asked, "How many times should I forgive someone who does something wrong to me? Is seven times enough?"

Jesus answered:

Not just seven times, but seventy-seven times! MATTHEW 18.21–22

If you forgive others for the wrongs they do to you, your Father in heaven will forgive you. But if you don't forgive others, your Father will not forgive your sins.

MATTHEW 6.14–15

Jesus said:

Don't judge others, and God won't judge you. Don't be hard on others, and God won't be hard on you. Forgive others, and God will forgive you.

LUKE 6.37

Whenever you stand up to pray, you must forgive what others have done to you. Then your Father in heaven will forgive your sins. MARK 11.25–26

Stop being bitter and angry and mad at others. Don't yell at one another or curse each other or ever be rude. Instead, be kind and merciful, and forgive others, just as God forgave you because of Christ.

EPHESIANS 4.31-32

Fellowship

🐾 You are better off to have a friend than to be all alone, because then you will get more enjoyment out of what you earn. If you fall, your friend can help you up. But if you fall without having a friend nearby, you are really in trouble.   ECCLESIASTES 4.9-10

They spent their time learning from the apostles, and they were like family to each other. They also broke bread and prayed together.

Everyone was amazed by the many miracles and wonders that the apostles worked. All the Lord's followers often met together, and they shared everything they had. They would sell their property and possessions and give the money to whoever needed it. Day after day they met together in the temple. They broke bread together in different homes and shared their food happily and freely.   ACTS 2.42–46

We enjoyed being together,
     and we went with others
     to your house, our God.   PSALM 55.14

We are telling you what we have seen and heard, so that you may share in this life with us. And we share in it with the Father and with his Son Jesus Christ. We are writing to tell you these things, because this makes us truly happy.   1 JOHN 1.3–4

Let the message about Christ completely fill your lives, while you use all your wisdom to teach and instruct each other. With thankful hearts, sing psalms, hymns, and spiritual songs to God. Whatever you say or do should be done in the name of the Lord Jesus, as you give thanks to God the Father because of him.
     COLOSSIANS 3.16–17

Holiness

❧ Who may climb the LORD's hill
or stand in his holy temple?
Only those who do right
for the right reasons,
and don't worship idols
or tell lies under oath.   PSALM 24.3-4

Then I will take away your stubbornness
and make you eager to be completely
faithful to me. You will want to obey me
and all my laws and teachings. You will
be my people, and I will be your God.
EZEKIEL 11.19-20

God blesses those people
whose hearts are pure.
They will see him!   MATTHEW 5.8

But now the name of our Lord Jesus
Christ and the power of God's Spirit have
washed you and made you holy and
acceptable to God.   1 CORINTHIANS 6.11

I pray that God, who gives peace, will
make you completely holy. And may your

spirit, soul, and body be kept healthy and faultless until our Lord Jesus Christ returns.   1 THESSALONIANS 5.23

The ones who stop doing evil and make themselves pure will become special. Their lives will be holy and pleasing to their Master, and they will be able to do all kinds of good deeds.   2 TIMOTHY 2.21

He gave himself to rescue us from everything that is evil and to make our hearts pure. He wanted us to be his own people and to be eager to do right.

TITUS 2.14

Victory over Sin

❧ Children, you belong to God, and you have defeated these enemies. God's Spirit is in you and is more powerful than the one that is in the world.   1 JOHN 4.4

And now that Jesus has suffered and was tempted, he can help anyone else who is tempted.   HEBREWS 2.18

What a miserable person I am. Who will rescue me from this body that is doomed to die? Thank God! Jesus Christ will rescue me.   ROMANS 7.24-25

Finally, let the mighty strength of the Lord make you strong. Put on all the armor that God gives, so you can defend yourself against the devil's tricks. We are not fighting against humans. We are fighting against forces and authorities and against rulers of darkness and powers in the spiritual world. So put on all the armor that God gives. Then when that evil day comes, you will be able to defend yourself. And when the battle is over, you will still be standing firm.   EPHESIANS 6.10-13

Surrender to God! Resist the devil, and he will run from you. Come near to God, and he will come near to you. Clean up your lives, you sinners.   JAMES 4.7-8

Be on your guard and stay awake. Your enemy, the devil, is like a roaring lion, sneaking around to find someone to attack.

But you must resist the devil and stay strong in your faith. You know that all over the world the Lord's followers are suffering just as you are.   1 PETER 5.8–9

Don't let sin keep ruling your lives. You are ruled by God's kindness and not by the Law.   ROMANS 6.14

Even if you think you can stand up to temptation, be careful not to fall. You are tempted in the same way that everyone else is tempted. But God can be trusted not to let you be tempted too much, and he will show you how to escape from your temptations.   1 CORINTHIANS 10.12–13

Finding What God Wants

❧ I will lead the blind on roads they have never known;
   I will guide them on paths
   they have never traveled.

Their road is dark and rough,
but I will give light
    to keep them from stumbling.
This is my solemn promise.   ISAIAH 42.16

    We often suffer, but we are never
crushed. Even when we don't know what to
do, we never give up. In times of trouble,
God is with us, and when we are knocked
down, we get up again.

2 CORINTHIANS 4.6

Search for wisdom
    as you would search for silver
    or hidden treasure.
Then you will understand
what it means to respect
    and to know the LORD God.

All wisdom comes from the LORD,
    and so do common sense
    and understanding.
God gives helpful advice
to everyone who obeys him
    and protects all of those
    who live as they should.

PROVERBS 2.4–7

When I asked for your help,
    you answered my prayer
    and gave me courage.   PSALM 138.3

With all your heart you must trust the LORD
    and not your own judgment.
Always let him lead you,
    and he will clear the road
    for you to follow.   PROVERBS 3.5-6

Your teachings are wonderful,
and I respect them all.
Understanding your word brings light
    to the minds of ordinary people.

PSALM 119.129-130

You said to me, "I will point out the road
    that you should follow.
I will be your teacher and watch over you."

PSALM 32.8

Safety

𝄞 When you cross deep rivers,
I will be with you,
    and you won't drown.

55

When you walk through fire,
you won't be burned
    or scorched by the flames.

ISAIAH 43.2

My sheep know my voice, and I know them. They follow me, and I give them eternal life, so that they will never be lost. No one can snatch them out of my hand. My Father gave them to me, and he is greater than all others. No one can snatch them from his hands, and I am one with the Father.   JOHN 10.27-30

At that time, people will say,
"The LORD has saved us!
Let's celebrate. We waited and hoped—
    now our God is here."   ISAIAH 25.9

In everything we have won more than a victory because of Christ who loves us. I am sure that nothing can separate us from God's love—not life or death, not angels or spirits, not the present or the future, and not powers above or powers below. Nothing in all creation can separate us from God's love for us in Christ Jesus our Lord!

ROMANS 8.37-39

56

The LORD gives me strength.
He makes my feet as sure
as those of a deer,
    and he helps me stand
    on the mountains.   HABAKKUK 3.19

When I felt my feet slipping,
    you came with your love
    and kept me steady.   PSALM 94.18

The Lord watches over everyone
who obeys him,
and he listens to their prayers.
    But he opposes everyone who does evil.
    Can anyone really harm you for being
eager to do good deeds?   1 PETER 3.12–13

Answered Prayer

Ask, and you will receive. Search, and
you will find. Knock, and the door will be
opened for you. Everyone who asks will
receive. Everyone who searches will find.
And the door will be opened for everyone
who knocks.   MATTHEW 7.7–8

I praise you, LORD!
   I prayed, and you rescued me
   from my enemies.   PSALM 18.3

I will answer their prayers
before they finish praying.   ISAIAH 65.24

When you are in trouble, call out to me.
I will answer and be there
to protect and honor you.   PSALM 91.15

The LORD has chosen
everyone who is faithful
to be his very own,
   and he answers my prayers.

                                    PSALM 4.3

   Stay joined to me and let my teachings
become part of you. Then you can pray for
whatever you want, and your prayer will be
answered.   JOHN 15.7

   Ask me, and I will do whatever you ask.
This way the Son will bring honor to the
Father. I will do whatever you ask me to do.

                                JOHN 14.13-14

If you have faith when you pray for sick people, they will get well. The Lord will heal them, and if they have sinned, he will forgive them.   JAMES 5.15

When that time comes, you won't have to ask me about anything. I tell you for certain that the Father will give you whatever you ask for in my name.

JOHN 16.23

Praise

❧ All of you nations,
come praise the LORD!
   Let everyone praise him.
His love for us is wonderful;
   his faithfulness never ends.
Shout praises to the LORD!   PSALM 117.1-2

Shout praises to the LORD! Our God is kind,
   and it is right and good
   to sing praises to him.   PSALM 147.1

59

It is wonderful to be grateful
    and to sing your praises,
    LORD Most High!
It is wonderful each morning
to tell about your love
    and at night to announce
    how faithful you are.
I enjoy praising your name
to the music of harps,
because everything you do
makes me happy,
    and I sing joyful songs.   PSALM 92.1-4

You, LORD, are my God!
I will praise you
for doing the wonderful things
    you had planned and promised
    since ancient times.   ISAIAH 25.1

But thank God for letting our Lord Jesus
Christ give us the victory!
                    1 CORINTHIANS 15.57

All of you faithful people,
praise our glorious Lord!
    Celebrate and worship.

Praise God with songs on your lips
    and a sword in your hand.

PSALM 149.5–6

I will praise the LORD God
    with a song and a thankful heart.

PSALM 69.30

Now sing praises to God!
    Every kingdom on earth,
    sing to the Lord!
Praise the one who rides
across the ancient skies;
    listen as he speaks with a mighty voice.

PSALM 68.32–33

Our sacrifice is to keep offering praise to God in the name of Jesus.

HEBREWS 13.15

Helping Others

Make your light shine, so that others will see the good that you do and will praise your Father in heaven. MATTHEW 5.16

And anyone who gives one of my most humble followers a cup of cool water, just because that person is my follower, will surely be rewarded.   MATTHEW 10.42

When I was hungry, you gave me something to eat, and when I was thirsty, you gave me something to drink. When I was a stranger, you welcomed me, and when I was naked, you gave me clothes to wear. When I was sick, you took care of me, and when I was in jail, you visited me.

Then the ones who pleased the Lord will ask, "When did we give you something to eat or drink? When did we welcome you as a stranger or give you clothes to wear or visit you while you were sick or in jail?"

The king will answer, "Whenever you did it for any of my people, no matter how unimportant they seemed, you did it for me."   MATTHEW 25.35-40

If you know someone who doesn't have any clothes or food, you shouldn't just say, "I hope all goes well for you. I hope you will be warm and have plenty to eat." What good is it to say this, unless you do something to help? Faith that doesn't lead us to do good deeds is all alone and dead!

JAMES 2.15-17

If we have all we need and see one of our own people in need, we must have pity on that person, or else we cannot say we love God.   1 JOHN 3.17

Children, you show love for others by truly helping them, and not merely by talking about it.   1 JOHN 3.18

God planned for us to do good things and to live as he has always wanted us to live. That's why he sent Christ to make us what we are.   EPHESIANS 2.10

But don't forget to help others and to share your possessions with them. This too is like offering a sacrifice that pleases God.

HEBREWS 13.16

God is always fair. He will remember how you helped his people in the past and how you are still helping them. You belong to God, and he won't forget the love you have shown his people.   HEBREWS 6.10

63

They will always be remembered
and greatly praised,
    because they were kind
    and freely gave to the poor.

PSALM 112.9

When you give a feast, invite the poor,
the crippled, the lame, and the blind. They
cannot pay you back. But God will bless you
and reward you when his people rise from
death.   LUKE 14.13-14

When you give to the poor, don't let
anyone know about it. Then your gift will be
given in secret. Your Father knows what is
done in secret, and he will reward you.

MATTHEW 6.3-4

Caring for the poor is lending to the LORD,
    and you will be well repaid.

PROVERBS 19.17

As long as I can remember,
good people have never
been left helpless,
    and their children have never
    gone begging for food.

They gladly give and lend,
    and their children turn out good.

PSALM 37.25-26

Managing God's Resources

🐝 Do your work willingly, as though you
were serving the Lord himself, and not just
your earthly master. In fact, the Lord Christ
is the one you are really serving, and you
know that he will reward you.

COLOSSIANS 3.23-24

Remember this saying,
    "A few seeds make a small harvest,
        but a lot of seeds make
        a big harvest."
Each of you must make up your own
mind about how much to give. But don't
feel sorry that you must give and don't feel
that you are forced to give. God loves
people who love to give. God can bless you
with everything you need, and you will

always have more than enough to do all
kinds of good things for others.

2 CORINTHIANS 9.6-8

Don't store up treasures on earth! Moths
and rust can destroy them, and thieves can
break in and steal them. Instead, store up
your treasures in heaven, where moths and
rust cannot destroy them, and thieves
cannot break in and steal them. Your heart
will always be where your treasure is.

MATTHEW 6.19-21

Sometimes you can become rich
by being generous
    or poor by being greedy.
Generosity will be rewarded:
Give a cup of water,
    and you will receive
    a cup of water in return.
Charge too much for grain,
and you will be cursed;
    sell it at a fair price,
    and you will be praised.
Try hard to do right,
and you will win friends;
    go looking for trouble,
    and you will find it.

Trust in your wealth,
and you will be a failure,
   but God's people will prosper
   like healthy plants.   PROVERBS 11.24-28

   When you collect money for God's
people, I want you to do exactly what I told
the churches in Galatia to do. That is, each
Sunday each of you must put aside part of
what you have earned. If you do this, you
won't have to take up a collection when I
come.   1 CORINTHIANS 16.1-2

Honor the LORD by giving him your money
   and the first part of all your crops.
Then you will have more grain and grapes
   than you will ever need.
                              PROVERBS 3.9-10

   God is always fair. He will remember
how you helped his people in the past and
how you are still helping them. You belong
to God, and he won't forget the love you
have shown his people.   HEBREWS 6.10

Obedience

❧ Our LORD, you bless everyone
who lives right and obeys your Law.
You bless all of those
who follow your commands
from deep in their hearts. PSALM 119.1-2

If you obey my laws and teachings, you
will live safely in the land and enjoy its
abundant crops. LEVITICUS 25.18-19

If you and your king want to be followers
of the LORD, you must worship him and do
what he says. Don't be stubborn! If you're
stubborn and refuse to obey the LORD, he
will turn against you and your king.
1 SAMUEL 12.14-15

You have a choice—do you want the
LORD to bless you, or do you want him to
put a curse on you? Today I am giving you
his laws, and if you obey him, he will bless
you. DEUTERONOMY 11.26-27

Now if you will faithfully obey me, you
will be my very own people. The whole world

is mine, but you will be my holy nation and serve me as priests.   EXODUS 19.5-6

If you love me, you will do what I have said, and my Father will love you. I will also love you and show you what I am like.

JOHN 14.21

Prayer

🐦 When you pray, go into a room alone and close the door. Pray to your Father in private. He knows what is done in private, and he will reward you.   MATTHEW 6.6

Our LORD, everything you do
is kind and thoughtful,
    and you are near to everyone
    whose prayers are sincere.
You satisfy the desires
of all your worshipers,
    and you come to save them
    when they ask for help.

PSALM 145.17-19

I promise that when any two of you
on earth agree about something you are
praying for, my Father in heaven will do it
for you. Whenever two or three of you come
together in my name, I am there with you.

MATTHEW 18.19-20

Please listen, LORD!
Answer my prayer for help.
When I am in trouble, I pray,
knowing you will listen. PSALM 86.6-7

Ask me, and I will tell you things that
you don't know and can't find out.

JEREMIAH 33.3

But without faith no one can please God.
We must believe that God is real and that he
rewards everyone who searches for him.

HEBREWS 11.6

Always be joyful and never stop praying.
Whatever happens, keep thanking God
because of Jesus Christ. This is what God
wants you to do. 1 THESSALONIANS 5.16-18

Sharing Your Faith

In the Scriptures it says, "I spoke because I had faith." We have that same kind of faith. So we speak because we know that God raised the Lord Jesus to life. And just as God raised Jesus, he will also raise us to life.   2 CORINTHIANS 4.13–14

So, when you accepted the message, you followed our example and the example of the Lord. You suffered, but the Holy Spirit made you glad.

You became an example for all the Lord's followers in Macedonia and Achaia. And because of you, the Lord's message has spread everywhere in those regions. Now the news of your faith in God is known all over the world, and we don't have to say a thing about it. Everyone is talking about how you welcomed us and how you turned away from idols to serve the true and living God.   1 THESSALONIANS 1.6–9

When the good news about the kingdom has been preached all over the world and told to all nations, the end will come.

MATTHEW 24.14

Honor Christ and let him be the Lord of your life.

Always be ready to give an answer when someone asks you about your hope. Give a kind and respectful answer and keep your conscience clear. This way you will make people ashamed for saying bad things about your good conduct as a follower of Christ. You are better off to obey God and suffer for doing right than to suffer for doing wrong.   1 PETER 3.15-17

Jesus came to them and said:

I have been given all authority in heaven and on earth! Go to the people of all nations and make them my disciples. Baptize them in the name of the Father, the Son, and the Holy Spirit, and teach them to do everything I have told you. I will be with you always, even until the end of the world.

MATTHEW 28.18-20

Improving Your Faith

🐌 Do your best to improve your faith. You can do this by adding goodness, understanding, self-control, patience, devotion to God, concern for others, and love. If you keep growing in this way, it will show that what you know about our Lord Jesus Christ has made your lives useful and meaningful. But if you don't grow, you are like someone who is nearsighted or blind, and you have forgotten that your past sins are forgiven. 2 PETER 1.5-9

The LORD hasn't lost his powerful strength;
    he can still hear and answer prayers.
Your sins are the roadblock
between you and your God.
That's why he doesn't answer your prayers
    or let you see his face. ISAIAH 59.1-2

You harvest what you plant,
whether good or bad. PROVERBS 14.14

Even if you think you can stand up to temptation, be careful not to fall. You are tempted in the same way that everyone else is tempted. But God can be trusted not to let you be tempted too much, and he will show you how to escape from your temptations. 1 CORINTHIANS 10.12-13

If we say that we have not sinned, we are fooling ourselves, and the truth isn't in our hearts. But if we confess our sins to God, he can always be trusted to forgive us and take our sins away.   1 JOHN 1.8–9

Don't blame God when you are tempted! God cannot be tempted by evil, and he doesn't use evil to tempt others. We are tempted by our own desires that drag us off and trap us. Our desires make us sin, and when sin is finished with us, it leaves us dead.   JAMES 1.13–15

Surrender to God! Resist the devil, and he will run from you. Come near to God, and he will come near to you. Clean up your lives, you sinners.   JAMES 4.7–8

God is the one who began this good work in you, and I am certain that he won't stop before it is complete on the day that Christ Jesus returns.   PHILIPPIANS 1.6

For Times of Loneliness

❧ Don't be afraid. I am with you.
    Don't tremble with fear. I am your God.
I will make you strong,
as I protect you with my arm
    and give you victories.   ISAIAH 41.10

    Jesus said to his disciples, "Don't be worried! Have faith in God and have faith in me."   JOHN 14.1

    In everything we have won more than a victory because of Christ who loves us. I am sure that nothing can separate us from God's love—not life or death, not angels or spirits, not the present or the future, and not powers above or powers below. Nothing in all creation can separate us from God's love for us in Christ Jesus our Lord!
                        ROMANS 8.37-39

I celebrate and shout because you are kind.
    You saw all my suffering,
        and you cared for me.   PSALM 31.7

Can anything separate us from the love of Christ? Can trouble, suffering, and hard times, or hunger and nakedness, or danger and death?   ROMANS 8.35

The LORD is good.
He protects those who trust him
    in times of trouble.   NAHUM 1.7

God cares for you, so turn all your worries over to him.   1 PETER 5.7

For Times of Fear

❧ The LORD will protect you
    and keep you safe from all dangers.
The LORD will protect you
    now and always wherever you go.
                PSALM 121.7-8

Live under the protection of God Most High
    and stay in the shadow
    of God All-Powerful.
Then you will say to the LORD,

"You are my fortress, my place of safety;
     you are my God, and I trust you."
                              PSALM 91.1–2

The LORD Most High is your fortress.
Run to him for safety,
     and no terrible disasters will strike you
     or your home.   PSALM 91.9–10

Don't fall into the trap of being a coward—
     trust the LORD, and you will be safe.
                              PROVERBS 29.25

God will command his angels
to protect you
     wherever you go.
They will carry you in their arms,
     and you won't hurt your feet
     on the stones.   PSALM 91.11–12

So don't be afraid of sudden disasters
     or storms that strike those who are evil.
You can be sure
     that the LORD will protect you
     from harm.   PROVERBS 3.25–26

The Lord helps me! Why should I be afraid
of what people can do to me?

HEBREWS 13.6

You are my hiding place!
You protect me from trouble,
and you put songs in my heart
because you have saved me.

PSALM 32.7

I may walk through valleys
as dark as death,
but I won't be afraid.
You are with me,
and your shepherd's rod
makes me feel safe.

You treat me to a feast,
while my enemies watch.
You honor me as your guest,
and you fill my cup until it overflows.

PSALM 23.4-5

God is our mighty fortress,
always ready to help in times of trouble.

PSALM 46.1

I give you peace, the kind of peace that only I can give. It isn't like the peace that this world can give. So don't be worried or afraid. JOHN 14.27

For Times of Anger

🕊 Only fools get angry quickly and hold a grudge. ECCLESIASTES 7.9

If you forgive others for the wrongs they do to you, your Father in heaven will forgive you. But if you don't forgive others, your Father will not forgive your sins.

MATTHEW 6.14–15

Dear friends, don't try to get even. Let God take revenge. In the Scriptures the Lord says,
> "I am the one to take revenge
> and pay them back."

ROMANS 12.19

It's smart to be patient,
> but it's stupid to lose your temper.

PROVERBS 14.29

Don't be angry or furious.
Anger can lead to sin.   PSALM 37.8

Don't get so angry that you sin. Don't
go to bed angry and don't give the devil a
chance.   EPHESIANS 4.26-27

Stop being bitter and angry and mad at
others. Don't yell at one another and curse
each other or ever be rude. Instead, be kind
and merciful, and forgive others, just as
God forgave you because of Christ.
EPHESIANS 4.31-32

For Times of Frustration

❧ Let the LORD lead you
and trust him to help.   PSALM 37.5

With all your heart you must trust the LORD
    and not your own judgment.
Always let him lead you,
    and he will clear the road
    for you to follow.   PROVERBS 3.5-6

But now you will again see the Lord,
your teacher, and he will guide you. Whether
you turn to the right or to the left, you will
hear a voice saying, "This is the road! Now
follow it." ISAIAH 30.20–21

But the LORD God keeps me
from being disgraced.
So I refuse to give up,
 because I know God will never
 let me down. ISAIAH 50.7

Don't worry about anything, but pray
about everything. With thankful hearts offer
up your prayers and requests to God. Then,
because you belong to Christ Jesus, God
will bless you with peace that no one can
completely understand. And this peace will
control the way you think and feel.

PHILIPPIANS 4.6–7

You said to me, "I will point out the road
 that you should follow.
I will be your teacher and watch over you."

PSALM 32.8

If you do what the LORD wants,
   he will make certain
   each step you take is sure.
The LORD will hold your hand,
   and if you stumble, you still won't fall.

PSALM 37.23-24

For Times of Guilt

🕊 Turn back to me! I have rescued you
   and swept away your sins
   as though they were clouds.

ISAIAH 44.22

The LORD won't always be angry
and point out our sins;
   he doesn't punish us
   as our sins deserve.

How great is God's love for all
who worship him?
   Greater than the distance
   between heaven and earth!

How far has the LORD taken
our sins from us?
Farther than the distance
from east to west! PSALM 103.9–12

Our God, no one is like you.
We are all that is left of your chosen people,
and you freely forgive our sin and guilt.
You don't stay angry forever;
you're glad to have pity
and pleased to be merciful.
You will trample on our sins
and throw them in the sea.

MICAH 7.18–19

Give up your crooked ways
and your evil thoughts.
Return to the LORD our God.
He will be merciful and forgive your sins.

ISAIAH 55.7

So I tell you that all her sins are forgiven,
and that is why she has shown great love.
But anyone who has been forgiven for only a
little will show only a little love.

Then Jesus said to the woman, "Your sins are forgiven." LUKE 7.47–48

The LORD God is kind and merciful, and if you turn back to him, he will no longer turn his back on you. 2 CHRONICLES 30.9

So I confessed my sins
and told them all to you.
   I said, "I'll tell the LORD
   each one of my sins."
Then you forgave me
and took away my guilt. PSALM 32.5

If we say that we have not sinned, we are fooling ourselves, and the truth isn't in our hearts. But if we confess our sins to God, he can always be trusted to forgive us and take our sins away. 1 JOHN 1.8–9

So let's come near God with pure hearts and a confidence that comes from having faith. Let's keep our hearts pure, our consciences free from evil, and our bodies washed with clean water. HEBREWS 10.22

For Times of Rebellion

Christ was humble. He obeyed God
and even died on a cross.
Then God gave Christ the highest place
and honored his name above all others.

PHILIPPIANS 2.8–9

Don't let sin rule your body. After all, your body is bound to die, so don't obey its desires or let any part of it become a slave of evil. Give yourselves to God, as people who have been raised from death to life. Make every part of your body a slave that pleases God.   ROMANS 6.12–13

Stop doing wrong and learn to live right.
See that justice is done.
Defend widows and orphans
and help those in need.

ISAIAH 1.16–17

You used to be like people living in the dark, but now you are people of the light because you belong to the Lord. So act like people of the light and make your light shine. Be good and honest and truthful, as you try to please the Lord. Don't take part in doing those worthless things that are done in the dark. Instead, show how wrong they are.   EPHESIANS 5.8-11

The Lord wants you to obey all human authorities, especially the Emperor, who rules over everyone. You must also obey governors, because they are sent by the Emperor to punish criminals and to praise good citizens.   1 PETER 2.13-14

All of you young people should obey your elders. In fact, everyone should be humble toward everyone else. The Scriptures say,
          "God opposes proud people,
               but he helps everyone
               who is humble."
Be humble in the presence of God's mighty power, and he will honor you when the time comes.   1 PETER 5.5-6

For Times of Suffering

🕭 We share in the terrible sufferings of Christ, but also in the wonderful comfort he gives. We suffer in the hope that you will be comforted and saved. And because we are comforted, you will also be comforted, as you patiently endure suffering like ours.

2 CORINTHIANS 1.5–6

You made me suffer a lot,
but you will bring me back from this deep pit
    and give me new life.
You will make me truly great
and take my sorrow away.

PSALM 71.20–21

Dear friends, don't be surprised or shocked that you are going through testing that is like walking through fire. Be glad for the chance to suffer as Christ suffered. It will prepare you for even greater happiness when he makes his glorious return.

Count it a blessing when you suffer for being a Christian. This shows that God's glorious Spirit is with you.

1 PETER 4.12–14

God's Spirit makes us sure that we are his children. His Spirit lets us know that together with Christ we will be given what God has promised. We will also share in the

87

glory of Christ, because we have suffered
with him.

I am sure that what we are suffering now
cannot compare with the glory that will be
shown to us.   ROMANS 8.16-18

Even if good people fall seven times,
    they will get back up.
But when trouble strikes the wicked,
    that's the end of them.

PROVERBS 24.16

You rescue the humble,
    but you put down all who are proud.

PSALM 18.27

But God will bless you, if you have to
suffer for doing something good. After all,
God chose you to suffer as you follow in the
footsteps of Christ, who set an example by
suffering for you.   1 PETER 2.20-21

If you are having trouble, you should
pray. And if you are feeling good, you
should sing praises.   JAMES 5.13

Trust the LORD! Be brave and strong
and trust the LORD.   PSALM 27.14

For Times of Discouragement

🐦 Keep on being brave! It will bring you great rewards. Learn to be patient, so that you will please God and be given what he has promised. HEBREWS 10.35-36

Jesus told him:

You can be sure that anyone who gives up home or brothers or sisters or mother or father or children or land for me and for the good news will be rewarded. In this world they will be given a hundred times as many houses and brothers and sisters and mothers and children and pieces of land, though they will also be mistreated. And in the world to come, they will have eternal life. MARK 10.29-30

Just as parents are kind to their children, the LORD is kind to all who worship him,
    because he knows we are made of dust.
                                  PSALM 103.13-14

We often suffer, but we are never crushed. Even when we don't know what to

do, we never give up. In times of trouble,
God is with us, and when we are knocked
down, we get up again.

2 CORINTHIANS 4.8-9

In everything we have won more than a
victory because of Christ who loves us. I
am sure that nothing can separate us from
God's love—not life or death, not angels or
spirits, not the present or the future, and
not powers above or powers below. Nothing
in all creation can separate us from God's
love for us in Christ Jesus our Lord!

ROMANS 8.37-39

God's home is now with his people. He
will live with them, and they will be his
own. Yes, God will make his home among
his people. He will wipe all tears from their
eyes, and there will be no more death,
suffering, crying, or pain. These things
of the past are gone forever.

REVELATION 21.3-4

Don't worry about anything, but pray
about everything. With thankful hearts offer
up your prayers and requests to God. Then,

because you belong to Christ Jesus, God will bless you with peace that no one can completely understand. And this peace will control the way you think and feel.

PHILIPPIANS 4.6–7

Jesus said to his disciples, "Don't be worried! Have faith in God and have faith in me." JOHN 14.1

For Times of Depression

When you cross deep rivers,
I will be with you,
    and you won't drown.
When you walk through fire,
you won't be burned
    or scorched by the flames.

ISAIAH 43.2

The LORD has sent me
to comfort those who mourn,
    especially in Jerusalem.

91

He sent me to give them
flowers in place of their sorrow,
olive oil in place of tears,
and joyous praise
in place of broken hearts.

ISAIAH 61.2–3

Now those you have rescued
will return to Jerusalem,
singing on their way.
They will be crowned with great happiness,
never again to be burdened
with sadness and sorrow.

ISAIAH 51.11

He renews our hopes and heals our bodies.

PSALM 147.3

For Times of Trouble

Praise God, the Father of our Lord
Jesus Christ! The Father is a merciful God,
who always gives us comfort. He comforts
us when we are in trouble, so that we can
share that same comfort with others in
trouble. 2 CORINTHIANS 1.3–4

You were in serious trouble,
    but you prayed to the LORD,
    and he rescued you.
By the power of his own word, he healed you
    and saved you from destruction.

You should praise the LORD for his love
    and for the wonderful things
    he does for all of us.   PSALM 107.19-21

The LORD is good.
He protects those who trust him
    in times of trouble.   NAHUM 1.7

I am surrounded by trouble,
    but you protect me
    against my angry enemies.
With your own powerful arm
you keep me safe.   PSALM 138.7

We trap ourselves by telling lies,
    but we stay out of trouble by living right.
We are rewarded or punished
for what we say and do.
Fools think they know what is best,
    but a sensible person listens to advice.
                  PROVERBS 12.13-15

You, LORD God, bless everyone
who cares for the poor,
    and you rescue those people
    in times of trouble.
You protect them and keep them alive.
You make them happy here in this land,
    and you don't hand them over
    to their enemies.
You always heal them
and restore their strength
    when they are sick. PSALM 41.1-3

God is our mighty fortress,
    always ready to help in times of trouble.
                    PSALM 46.1

God will protect you from harm,
    no matter how often trouble may strike.
                    JOB 5.19

I give you peace, the kind of peace that
only I can give. It isn't like the peace that
this world can give. So don't be worried or
afraid. JOHN 14.27

For Times of Need

You, LORD, are my shepherd.
I will never be in need.   PSALM 23.1

God rescues the needy
from the words of the wicked
    and the fist of the mighty.
The poor are filled with hope,
    and injustice is silenced.   JOB 5.15–16

Fig trees may no longer bloom,
    or vineyards produce grapes;
olive trees may be fruitless,
    and harvest time a failure;
sheep pens may be empty,
    and cattle stalls vacant—
but I will still celebrate
    because the LORD God saves me.

                    HABAKKUK 3.17–18

I will protect you from anything that
makes you unclean. Your fields will overflow
with grain, and no one will starve. Your
trees will be filled with fruit, and crops will
grow in your fields, so that you will never

again feel ashamed for not having enough
food.   EZEKIEL 36.29-30

I, the LORD, am the one
who sends storm clouds
    and showers of rain
    to make fields produce.
So when the crops need rain,
you should pray to me.   ZECHARIAH 10.1

God lifts the poor and needy
from dust and ashes,
    and he lets them take part
    in ruling his people.   PSALM 113.7-8

My dear friends, pay attention. God has
given a lot of faith to the poor people in this
world. He has also promised them a share
in his kingdom that he will give to everyone
who loves him.   JAMES 2.5

For Times of Temptation

🐚 I pray that God the Father and our
Lord Jesus Christ will be kind to you and
will bless you with peace! Christ obeyed

God our Father and gave himself as a
sacrifice for our sins to rescue us from
this evil world.   GALATIANS 1.3-4

Be on your guard and stay awake. Your
enemy, the devil, is like a roaring lion,
sneaking around to find someone to attack.
But you must resist the devil and stay
strong in your faith. You know that all over
the world the Lord's followers are suffering
just as you are.   1 PETER 5.8-9

Don't blame God when you are tempted!
God cannot be tempted by evil, and he
doesn't use evil to tempt others. We are
tempted by our own desires that drag us off
and trap us. Our desires make us sin, and
when sin is finished with us, it leaves us
dead.   JAMES 1.13-15

Even if you think you can stand up to
temptation, be careful not to fall. You are
tempted in the same way that everyone else
is tempted. But God can be trusted not
to let you be tempted too much, and he
will show you how to escape from your
temptations.   1 CORINTHIANS 10.12-13

My friends, be glad, even if you have a lot of trouble. You know that you learn to endure by having your faith tested.

JAMES 1.2-3

He will give eternal life to everyone who has patiently done what is good in the hope of receiving glory, honor, and life that lasts forever. ROMANS 2.7

And now that Jesus has suffered and was tempted, he can help anyone else who is tempted. HEBREWS 2.18

Finally, let the mighty strength of the Lord make you strong. Put on all the armor that God gives, so you can defend yourself against the devil's tricks. We are not fighting against humans. We are fighting against forces and authorities and against rulers of darkness and powers in the spiritual world. So put on all the armor that God gives. Then when that evil day comes, you will be able to defend yourself. And when the battle is over, you will still be standing firm. EPHESIANS 6.10-13

For Times of Impatience

🐚 And the Scriptures were written to teach and encourage us by giving us hope. God is the one who makes us patient and cheerful. I pray that he will help you live at peace with each other, as you follow Christ.

ROMANS 15.4–5

I patiently waited, LORD,
for you to hear my prayer.
You listened and pulled me from a lonely pit
full of mud and mire.
You let me stand on a rock
with my feet firm,
and you gave me a new song,
a song of praise to you.
Many will see this, and they will honor
and trust you, the LORD God.

PSALM 40.1–3

My friends, be patient until the Lord returns. Think of farmers who wait patiently for the spring and summer rains to make their valuable crops grow. Be patient like those farmers and don't give up. The Lord will soon be here. JAMES 5.7–8

Be patient and trust the LORD.
Don't let it bother you
when all goes well for those
    who do sinful things.   PSALM 37.7

For Times of Sickness

❧ I will praise you, LORD!
You saved me from the grave
    and kept my enemies
    from celebrating my death.
I prayed to you, LORD God,
and you healed me,
    saving me from death and the grave.
                  PSALM 30.1-3

The LORD forgives our sins,
heals us when we are sick,
    and protects us from death.
His kindness and love
are a crown on our heads.
Each day that we live,
he provides for our needs
    and gives us the strength
    of a young eagle.   PSALM 103.3-5

Then someday, I will heal this place and my people as well, and let them enjoy unending peace.   JEREMIAH 33.6

A woman who had been bleeding for twelve years came up behind Jesus and barely touched his clothes. She had said to herself, "If I can just touch his clothes, I will get well."

Jesus turned. He saw the woman and said, "Don't worry! You are now well because of your faith." At that moment she was healed.   MATTHEW 9.20-22

If you are sick, ask the church leaders to come and pray for you. Ask them to put olive oil on you in the name of the Lord.
JAMES 5.14

Let's return to the LORD.
He has torn us to shreds,
    but he will bandage our wounds
    and make us well.
In two or three days he will heal us
    and restore our strength
    that we may live with him.
HOSEA 6.1-2

You, LORD, are the one I praise.
So heal me and rescue me!
    Then I will be completely well
    and perfectly safe.   JEREMIAH 17.14

You were in serious trouble,
    but you prayed to the LORD,
    and he rescued you.
By the power of his own word, he healed you
    and saved you from destruction.
                    PSALM 107.19–20

Knowing these teachings
    will mean true life
    and good health for you.
                    PROVERBS 4.22

For Times of Sadness

God blesses those people who grieve.
They will find comfort!   MATTHEW 5.4

We share in the terrible sufferings of
Christ, but also in the wonderful comfort he
gives. We suffer in the hope that you will be
comforted and saved. And because we are

comforted, you will also be comforted, as
you patiently endure suffering like ours.

2 CORINTHIANS 1.5-6

Even if my father and mother
should desert me,
    you will take care of me. PSALM 27.10

    God our Father loves us. He is kind
and has given us eternal comfort and a
wonderful hope. We pray that our Lord Jesus
Christ and God our Father will encourage
you and help you always to do and say the
right thing. 2 THESSALONIANS 2.16-17

For Times of Bereavement

🙿 I may walk through valleys
as dark as death,
    but I won't be afraid.
You are with me,
    and your shepherd's rod
    makes me feel safe.

You treat me to a feast,
while my enemies watch.
You honor me as your guest,
    and you fill my cup until it overflows.

PSALM 23.4–5

You are deeply concerned
    when one of your loyal people
    faces death.

I worship you, LORD, just as my mother did,
    and you have rescued me
    from the chains of death.

PSALM 116.15–16

As long as we are in these bodies, we are away from the Lord. But we live by faith, not by what we see. We should be cheerful, because we would rather leave these bodies and be at home with the Lord.

2 CORINTHIANS 5.6–8

Our bodies are like tents that we live in here on earth. But when these tents are destroyed, we know that God will give each of us a place to live. These homes will not be buildings that someone has made, but they are in heaven and will last forever.

While we are here on earth, we sigh because we want to live in that heavenly home. We want to put it on like clothes and not be naked.

These tents we now live in are like a heavy burden, and we groan. But we don't do this just because we want to leave these bodies that will die. It is because we want to change them for bodies that will never die. God is the one who makes all of this possible. He has given us his Spirit to make us certain that he will do it.

2 CORINTHIANS 5.1-5

The bodies we now have are weak and can die. But they will be changed into bodies that are eternal. Then the Scriptures will come true,

"Death has lost the battle!
Where is its victory?
Where is its sting?"

1 CORINTHIANS 15.54-55

God blesses those people who grieve. They will find comfort! MATTHEW 5.4

God's home is now with his people. He will live with them, and they will be his

105

own. Yes, God will make his home among his people. He will wipe all tears from their eyes, and there will be no more death, suffering, crying, or pain. These things of the past are gone forever.

REVELATION 21.3-4

Jesus then said, "I am the one who raises the dead to life! Everyone who has faith in me will live, even if they die. And everyone who lives because of faith in me will never really die." JOHN 11.25-26

Wives

❧ A truly good wife
is the most precious treasure
    a man can find!
Her husband depends on her,
    and she never lets him down.
She is good to him every day of her life,
    and with her own hands
    she gladly makes clothes.

She is like a sailing ship
    that brings food from across the sea.
She gets up before daylight to prepare food
    for her family and for her servants.
She knows how to buy land
and how to plant a vineyard,
    and she always works hard.
She knows when to buy or sell,
    and she stays busy until late at night.
She spins her own cloth,
    and she helps the poor and the needy.
Her family has warm clothing,
    and so she doesn't worry when it snows.

She does her own sewing,
    and everything she wears is beautiful.

Her husband is a well-known
and respected leader
    in the city.
She makes clothes to sell
to the shop owners.
She is strong and graceful,
    as well as cheerful about the future.
Her words are sensible,
    and her advice is thoughtful.
She takes good care of her family
and is never lazy.
Her children praise her,
    and with great pride her husband says,
"There are many good women,
but you are the best!"

Charm can be deceiving,
and beauty fades away,
but a woman who honors the LORD
    deserves to be praised.
Show her respect—
    praise her in public
    for what she has done.

PROVERBS 31.10–31

A wife belongs to her husband instead of to herself, and a husband belongs to his wife instead of to himself.

1 CORINTHIANS 7.4

You may inherit all you own
from your parents,
    but a sensible wife
    is a gift from the LORD.   PROVERBS 19.14

A man's greatest treasure is his wife—
    she is a gift from the LORD.

PROVERBS 18.22

Husbands

You should be faithful to your wife,
    just as you take water
    from your own well.
And don't be like a stream
    from which just any woman
    may take a drink.
Save yourself for your wife
    and don't have sex with other women.
Be happy with the wife you married
    when you were young.

109

She is beautiful and graceful,
just like a deer;
    you should be attracted to her
    and stay deeply in love.

PROVERBS 5.15–19

Life is short, and you love your wife, so
enjoy being with her. This is what you are
supposed to do as you struggle through life
on this earth.   ECCLESIASTES 9.9

A husband should love his wife as much
as Christ loved the church and gave his life
for it. He made the church holy by the power
of his word, and he made it pure by washing
it with water. Christ did this, so that he
would have a glorious and holy church,
without faults or spots or wrinkles or any
other flaws.

In the same way, a husband should love
his wife as much as he loves himself. A
husband who loves his wife shows that he
loves himself. None of us hate our own
bodies. We provide for them and take good
care of them, just as Christ does for the
church, because we are each part of his
body. As the Scriptures say, "A man leaves
his father and mother to get married, and

he becomes like one person with his wife."
This is a great mystery, but I understand it
to mean Christ and his church. So each
husband should love his wife as much as he
loves himself, and each wife should respect
her husband.   EPHESIANS 5.25-33

A husband must love his wife and not
abuse her.   COLOSSIANS 3.19

Parents

🐚 The LORD will love you and bless you by
giving you many children and plenty of food,
wine, and olive oil.   DEUTERONOMY 7.13

Grandparents are proud
of their grandchildren,
    and children should be proud
    of their parents.   PROVERBS 17.6

Correct your children, and they will be wise;
    children out of control
    disgrace their mothers.

If you correct your children,
   they will bring you peace and happiness.
                                        PROVERBS 29.15,17

   He will lead children and parents to love
each other more, so that when I come, I
won't bring doom to the land.
                                        MALACHI 4.6

Teach your children right from wrong,
   and when they are grown
   they will still do right.   PROVERBS 22.6

I pray that the LORD will let your family
   and your descendants
   always grow strong.
May the LORD who created
the heavens and the earth
   give you his blessing.   PSALM 115.14-15

   Parents, don't be hard on your children.
Raise them properly. Teach them and
instruct them about the Lord.
                                        EPHESIANS 6.4

   Parents, don't be hard on your children.
If you are, they might give up.
                                        COLOSSIANS 3.21

Children are a blessing
and a gift from the LORD.
Having a lot of children
to take care of you in your old age
    is like a warrior with a lot of arrows.
The more you have,
the better off you will be,
because they will protect you
    when your enemies attack
      with arguments.   PSALM 127.3-5

Children

Pay attention to your father,
    and don't neglect your mother
    when she grows old.
Invest in truth and wisdom,
discipline and good sense,
    and don't part with them.
Make your father truly happy by living right
    and showing sound judgment.
Make your parents proud,
especially your mother.

PROVERBS 23.22-25

113

Grandparents are proud
of their grandchildren,
    and children should be proud
    of their parents. PROVERBS 17.6

    Respect your father and mother, and you
will live a long and successful life in the
land I am giving you. DEUTERONOMY 5.16

Obey the teaching of your parents—
    always keep it in mind
    and never forget it.
Their teaching will guide you
when you walk,
protect you when you sleep,
    and talk to you
    when you are awake.

                PROVERBS 6.20–22

Young people can live a clean life
    by obeying your word. PSALM 119.9

    Children, you belong to the Lord, and
you do the right thing when you obey your
parents. The first commandment with a
promise says, "Obey your father and
mother, and you will have a long and
happy life." EPHESIANS 6.1–3

Marital Problems

𝄞 You obeyed the truth, and your souls were made pure. Now you sincerely love each other. But you must keep on loving with all your heart.   1 PETER 1.22

Love each other as brothers and sisters and honor others more than you do yourself. Never give up.   ROMANS 12.10-11

Hatred stirs up trouble;
    love overlooks the wrongs that others do.
                                PROVERBS 10.12

Divorce

𝄞 I instruct married couples to stay together, and this is exactly what the Lord himself taught. A wife who leaves her husband should either stay single or go back to her husband. And a husband should not leave his wife.

I don't know of anything else the Lord said about marriage. All I can do is to give you my own advice. If your wife isn't a follower of the Lord, but is willing to stay with you, don't divorce her. If your husband isn't a follower, but is willing to stay with you, don't divorce him. Your husband or wife who isn't a follower is made holy by having you as a mate. This also makes your children holy and keeps them from being unclean in God's sight.   1 CORINTHIANS 7.10–14

Some Pharisees wanted to test Jesus. So they came up to him and asked if it was right for a man to divorce his wife. Jesus asked them, "What does the Law of Moses say about that?"

They answered, "Moses allows a man to write out divorce papers and send his wife away."

Jesus replied, "Moses gave you this law because you are so heartless. But in the beginning God made a man and a woman. That's why a man leaves his father and mother and gets married. He becomes like one person with his wife. Then they are no longer two people, but one. And no one should separate a couple that God has joined together."   MARK 10.2-9

Desertion

❧ But I can be trusted
to care for your orphans and widows.

JEREMIAH 49.11

When the poor and needy are dying of thirst
    and cannot find water,
I, the LORD God of Israel,
will come to their rescue.
    I won't forget them.   ISAIAH 41.17

Why am I discouraged? Why am I restless?
I trust you! And I will praise you again
    because you help me,
    and you are my God.   PSALM 43.5

The LORD answered,
"Could a mother forget a child
    who nurses at her breast?
Could she fail to love an infant
    who came from her own body?
Even if a mother could forget,
I will never forget you.
A picture of your city is drawn on my hand.
    You are always in my thoughts!"

ISAIAH 49.15–16

The LORD defends the rights of orphans and widows. He cares for foreigners and gives them food and clothing.

DEUTERONOMY 10.18

The LORD your God will have mercy—he won't destroy you or desert you. The LORD will remember his promise, and he will keep the agreement he made with your ancestors.   DEUTERONOMY 4.31

God cares for you, so turn all your worries over to him.   1 PETER 5.7

Even if my father and mother
should desert me,
    you will take care of me.   PSALM 27.10

Financial Stress

❧ Honor the LORD!
You are his special people.
    No one who honors the LORD
    will ever be in need.

118

Young lions may go hungry or even starve,
but if you trust the LORD,
    you will never miss out
    on anything good.   PSALM 34.9-10

    But more than anything else, put God's
work first and do what he wants. Then the
other things will be yours as well.

MATTHEW 6.33

    The LORD will make your businesses and
your farms successful.
    You will have many children. You will
harvest large crops, and your herds of cattle
and flocks of sheep and goats will produce
many young.
    You will have plenty of bread to eat.
    The LORD will make you successful in
your daily work.
    The LORD will help you defeat your
enemies and make them scatter in all
directions.
    The LORD your God is giving you the
land, and he will make sure you are
successful in everything you do. Your
harvests will be so large that your
storehouses will be full.

DEUTERONOMY 28.3-8

In fact, everything is yours, including the world, life, death, the present, and the future. Everything belongs to you, and you belong to Christ, and Christ belongs to God.   1 CORINTHIANS 3.22-23

You, LORD, are my shepherd.
I will never be in need.   PSALM 23.1

I pray that God will take care of all your needs with the wonderful blessings that come from Christ Jesus!   PHILIPPIANS 4.19

Marriage

❧ The Lord God said, "It isn't good for the man to live alone. I need to make a suitable partner for him."

That's why a man will leave his own father and mother. He marries a woman, and the two of them become like one person.　GENESIS 2.18,24

Jesus answered, "Don't you know that in the beginning the Creator made a man and a woman? That's why a man leaves his father and mother and gets married. He becomes like one person with his wife. Then they are no longer two people, but one. And no one should separate a couple that God has joined together."　MATTHEW 19.4-6

Charm can be deceiving,
and beauty fades away,
but a woman who honors the Lord
　　deserves to be praised.

Show her respect—
  praise her in public
  for what she has done.
PROVERBS 31.30-31

A truly good wife
is the most precious treasure
  a man can find!
Her husband depends on her,
  and she never lets him down.
She is good to him every day of her life.
PROVERBS 31.10-12

A helpful wife is a jewel for her husband,
  but a shameless wife
  will make his bones rot.
PROVERBS 12.4

Have respect for marriage. Always be
faithful to your partner, because God will
punish anyone who is immoral or unfaithful
in marriage. HEBREWS 13.4

Business

❧ The LORD will bless you
  if you respect him and obey his laws.

Business

Your fields will produce,
   and you will be happy
   and all will go well.   PSALM 128.1–2

My people will live
in the houses they build;
   they will enjoy grapes
   from their own vineyards.
No one will take away
their homes or vineyards.
My chosen people will live
to be as old as trees,
   and they will enjoy
   what they have earned.
Their work won't be wasted.

                              ISAIAH 65.21–23

   If you obey him, he will send rain at the
right seasons, so you will have more than
enough food, wine, and olive oil, and there
will be plenty of grass for your cattle.

                    DEUTERONOMY 11.13–15

Share your plans with the LORD,
and you will succeed.   PROVERBS 16.3

The LORD doesn't like it
when we cheat in business.   PROVERBS 16.11

The LORD will give you a lot of children and make sure that your animals give birth to many young. The LORD promised your ancestors that this land would be yours, and he will make it produce large crops for you.

The LORD will open the storehouses of the skies where he keeps the rain, and he will send rain on your land at just the right times. He will make you successful in everything you do. You will have plenty of money to lend to other nations, but you won't need to borrow any yourself.

DEUTERONOMY 28.11-12

The Lord will send rain to water the seeds you have planted—your fields will produce more crops than you need, and your cattle will graze in open pastures. Even the oxen and donkeys that plow your fields will be fed the finest grain.

ISAIAH 30.23-24

Social

❦ But I am giving you a new command. You must love each other, just as I have loved you. If you love each other, everyone will know that you are my disciples.

JOHN 13.34-35

God's kingdom isn't about eating and drinking. It is about pleasing God, about living in peace, and about true happiness. All this comes from the Holy Spirit. If you serve Christ in this way, you will please God and be respected by people. We should try to live at peace and help each other have a strong faith. ROMANS 14.17-19

"When I was hungry, you gave me something to eat, and when I was thirsty, you gave me something to drink. When I was a stranger, you welcomed me, and when I was naked, you gave me clothes to wear. When I was sick, you took care of me, and when I was in jail, you visited me."

Then the ones who pleased the Lord will ask, "When did we give you something to eat or drink? When did we welcome you as a stranger or give you clothes to wear or visit you while you were sick or in jail?"

The king will answer, "Whenever you did it for any of my people, no matter how unimportant they seemed, you did it for me." MATTHEW 25.35-40

You are like light for the whole world. A city built on top of a hill cannot be hidden, and no one would light a lamp and put it under a clay pot. A lamp is placed on a lampstand, where it can give light to everyone in the house. Make your light shine, so that others will see the good that you do and will praise your Father in heaven. MATTHEW 5.14-16

And the Scriptures were written to teach and encourage us by giving us hope. God is the one who makes us patient and cheerful. I pray that he will help you live at peace with each other, as you follow Christ.
ROMANS 15.4-5

Let love be your only debt! If you love others, you have done all that the Law demands. In the Law there are many commands, such as, "Be faithful in marriage. Do not murder. Do not steal. Do not want what belongs to others." But all of these are summed up in the command that says, "Love others as much as you love yourself." No one who loves others will harm them. So love is all that the Law demands.

ROMANS 13.8-10

God loves you and has chosen you as his own special people. So be gentle, kind, humble, meek, and patient. Put up with each other, and forgive anyone who does you wrong, just as Christ has forgiven you. Love is more important than anything else. It is what ties everything completely together. COLOSSIANS 3.12-14

Church

ﻌ I want you to know about the great and mighty power that God has for us followers. It is the same wonderful power he used when he raised Christ from death and let him sit at his right side in heaven. There Christ rules over all forces, authorities, powers, and rulers. He rules over all beings in this world and will rule in the future world as well. God has put all things under the power of Christ, and for the good of the church he has made him the head of

127

everything. The church is Christ's body and is filled with Christ who completely fills everything.   EPHESIANS 1.20–23

The church in Judea, Galilee, and Samaria now had a time of peace and kept on worshiping the Lord. The church became stronger, as the Holy Spirit encouraged it and helped it grow.

ACTS 9.31

The group of followers all felt the same way about everything. None of them claimed that their possessions were their own, and they shared everything they had with each other. In a powerful way the apostles told everyone that the Lord Jesus was now alive. God greatly blessed his followers, and no one went in need of anything. Everyone who owned land or houses would sell them and bring the money to the apostles. Then they would give the money to anyone who needed it.

ACTS 4.32–35

Simon Peter spoke up, "You are the Messiah, the Son of the living God."
Jesus told him:

Simon, son of Jonah, you are blessed!
You didn't discover this on your own. It
was shown to you by my Father in
heaven. So I will call you Peter, which
means "a rock." On this rock I will build
my church, and death itself will not have
any power over it. I will give you the keys
to the kingdom of heaven, and God in
heaven will allow whatever you allow on
earth. But he will not allow anything that
you don't allow.   MATTHEW 16.16-19

Christ chose some of us to be apostles,
prophets, missionaries, pastors, and teachers,
so that his people would learn to serve and
his body would grow strong. This will continue
until we are united by our faith and by our
understanding of the Son of God. Then we
will be mature, just as Christ is, and we will
be completely like him.   EPHESIANS 4.11-13

But I am giving you a new command.
You must love each other, just as I have
loved you. If you love each other, everyone
will know that you are my disciples.

JOHN 13.34-35

Government

❧ Our God, your name
will be praised forever and forever.
     You are all-powerful,
     and you know everything.
You control human events—
you give rulers their power and take it away,
     and you are the source
     of wisdom and knowledge.

DANIEL 2.20-21

Obey the rulers who have authority over
you. Only God can give authority to anyone,
and he puts these rulers in their places of
power. People who oppose the authorities
are opposing what God has done, and they
will be punished. Rulers are a threat to evil
people, not to good people. There is no
need to be afraid of the authorities. Just do
right, and they will praise you for it. After
all, they are God's servants, and it is their
duty to help you.
     If you do something wrong, you ought
to be afraid, because these rulers have

the right to punish you. They are God's servants who punish criminals to show how angry God is. But you should obey the rulers because you know it is the right thing to do, and not just because of God's anger.

You must also pay your taxes. The authorities are God's servants, and it is their duty to take care of these matters. Pay all that you owe, whether it is taxes and fees or respect and honor.

ROMANS 13.1–7

Kings who are fair to the poor
will rule forever.   PROVERBS 29.14

Rulers are protected
by God's mercy and loyalty,
    but they must be merciful
    for their kingdoms to last.

PROVERBS 20.28

The Lord wants you to obey all human authorities, especially the Emperor, who rules over everyone. You must also obey

governors, because they are sent by the
Emperor to punish criminals and to praise
good citizens.   1 PETER 2.13-14

Unbelieving Loved Ones

❧ You are like light for the whole world. A
city built on top of a hill cannot be hidden,
and no one would light a lamp and put it
under a clay pot. A lamp is placed on a
lampstand, where it can give light to
everyone in the house. Make your light
shine, so that others will see the good that
you do and will praise your Father in
heaven.   MATTHEW 5.14-16

If your husband or wife isn't a follower of
the Lord and decides to divorce you, then
you should agree to it. You are no longer
bound to that person. After all, God chose
you and wants you to live at peace. And
besides, how do you know if you will be able
to save your husband or wife who isn't a
follower?   1 CORINTHIANS 7.15-16

They replied, "Have faith in the Lord Jesus and you will be saved! This is also true for everyone who lives in your home."

ACTS 16.31

If you are a wife, you must put your husband first. Even if he opposes our message, you will win him over by what you do. No one else will have to say anything to him, because he will see how you honor God and live a pure life. 1 PETER 3.1-2

Always let others see you behaving properly, even though they may still accuse you of doing wrong. Then on the day of judgment, they will honor God by telling the good things they saw you do.

1 PETER 2.12

The Lord isn't slow about keeping his promises, as some people think he is. In fact, God is patient, because he wants everyone to turn from sin and no one to be lost. 2 PETER 3.9

The Elderly

Young people take pride
in their strength,
but the gray hairs of wisdom
are even more beautiful.

PROVERBS 20.29

My child, remember
my teachings and instructions
and obey them completely.
They will help you live
a long and prosperous life.

PROVERBS 3.1-2

Good people will prosper like palm trees,
and they will grow strong
like the cedars of Lebanon.
They will take root in your house, LORD God,
and they will do well.
They will be like trees
that stay healthy and fruitful,
even when they are old.
And they will say about you,
"The LORD always does right!
God is our mighty rock."

PSALM 92.12-15

Gray hair is a glorious crown
    worn by those who have lived right.

PROVERBS 16.31

You have taught me since I was a child,
    and I never stop telling
    about your marvelous deeds.
Don't leave me when I am old
and my hair turns gray.
    Let me tell future generations
    about your mighty power.
Your deeds of kindness
are known in the heavens.
    No one is like you!   PSALM 71.17-19

I will still be the same
when you are old and gray,
    and I will take care of you.
I created you. I will carry you
    and always keep you safe.

ISAIAH 46.4

I am Wisdom.
    If you follow me, you will live a long time.

PROVERBS 9.11

Your home will be secure,
and your sheep will be safe.
You will have more descendants
    than there are blades of grass
    on the face of the earth.
You will live a long life,
    and your body will be strong
    until the day you die.   JOB 5.24–26

God's Faithfulness

❧ The LORD will lead you into the land. He will always be with you and help you, so don't ever be afraid of your enemies.

DEUTERONOMY 31.8

You know that the LORD your God is the only true God. So love him and obey his commands, and he will faithfully keep his agreement with you and your descendants for a thousand generations.

DEUTERONOMY 7.9

Your love is faithful, LORD,
    and even the clouds in the sky
    can depend on you. PSALM 36.5

The LORD is your protector,
    and he won't go to sleep
    or let you stumble.
The protector of Israel doesn't doze
or ever get drowsy. PSALM 121.3-4

I once promised Noah
that I would never again
   destroy the earth by a flood.
Now I have promised that I will never again
   get angry and punish you.
Every mountain and hill may disappear.
But I will always be kind
and merciful to you. ISAIAH 54.9–10

My body and mind may fail,
   but you are my strength
   and my choice forever. PSALM 73.26

   God can be trusted, and he chose you
to be partners with his Son, our Lord Jesus
Christ. 1 CORINTHIANS 1.9

Don't be afraid. I am with you.
   Don't tremble with fear. I am your God.
I will make you strong,
as I protect you with my arm
   and give you victories. ISAIAH 41.10

   When I see the rainbow in the sky, I will
always remember the promise that I have

made to every living creature. The rainbow will be the sign of that solemn promise.

GENESIS 9.16–17

Our LORD, I will sing of your love forever.
Everyone yet to be born
    will hear me praise your faithfulness.
I will tell them,
"God's love can always be trusted,
    and his faithfulness lasts
    as long as the heavens."

PSALM 89.1–2

The Lord isn't slow about keeping his promises, as some people think he is. In fact, God is patient, because he wants everyone to turn from sin and no one to be lost.   2 PETER 3.9

Victory of the Church

🕊 You are like a building with the apostles and prophets as the foundation and with Christ as the most important stone. Christ is the one who holds the building together and makes it grow into a

holy temple for the Lord. And you are part
of that building Christ has built as a place
for God's own Spirit to live.

EPHESIANS 2.20-22

After all, the church of the living God is
the strong foundation of truth.
 Here is the great mystery of our religion:
  Christ came as a human.
  The Spirit proved that he pleased God,
   and he was seen by angels.

  Christ was preached to the nations.
  People in this world
  put their faith in him,
   and he was taken up to glory.

1 TIMOTHY 3.15-16

In the future, the mountain
with the Lord's temple
 will be the highest of all.
It will reach above the hills;
every nation will rush to it.
Many people will come and say,
"Let's go to the mountain
of the Lord God of Jacob
 and worship in his temple."

ISAIAH 2.2-3

140

Our LORD, the nations will honor you,
    and all kings on earth
    will praise your glory.
You will rebuild the city of Zion.
Your glory will be seen,
    and the prayers of the homeless
    will be answered. PSALM 102.15–17

I pray that you will be grateful to God
for letting you have part in what he has
promised his people in the kingdom of
light. God rescued us from the dark power
of Satan and brought us into the kingdom
of his dear Son, who forgives our sins and
sets us free. COLOSSIANS 1.12–14

I pray that Christ Jesus and the church
will forever bring praise to God. His power
at work in us can do far more than we dare
ask or imagine. EPHESIANS 3.20–21

I did not see a temple there. The Lord
God All-Powerful and the Lamb were its
temple. And the city did not need the sun or
the moon. The glory of God was shining on
it, and the Lamb was its light.

Nations will walk by the light of that city, and kings will bring their riches there. Its gates are always open during the day, and night never comes. The glorious treasures of nations will be brought into the city. But nothing unworthy will be allowed to enter. No one who is dirty-minded or who tells lies will be there. Only those whose names are written in the Lamb's book of life will be in the city. REVELATION 21.22–27

God's Mercy in Judgment

I will gather you from the foreign nations and bring you home. I will sprinkle you with clean water, and you will be clean and acceptable to me. I will wash away everything that makes you unclean, and I will remove your disgusting idols. I will take away your stubborn heart and give you a new heart and a desire to be faithful. You will have only pure thoughts, because I will put my Spirit in you and make you eager to obey my laws and teachings. You will once

again live in the land I gave your ancestors;
you will be my people, and I will be your
God.   EZEKIEL 36.24-28

Jeremiah, you say that this land is a
desert without people or animals, and for
now, you are right. The towns of Judah and
the streets of Jerusalem are deserted, and
people and animals are nowhere to be seen.
But someday you will hear happy voices
and the sounds of parties and wedding
celebrations. And when people come to my
temple to offer sacrifices to thank
me, you will hear them say:
> "We praise you, LORD All-Powerful!
>> You are good to us,
>> and your love never fails."

JEREMIAH 33.10-11

I'll punish her for the days
she worshiped Baal
   and burned incense to him.
I'll punish her for the times
she forgot about me
   and wore jewelry and rings
   to attract her lovers.
I, the LORD, have spoken!

Israel, I, the LORD, will lure you
into the desert
   and speak gently to you.
I will return your vineyards,
and then Trouble Valley
   will become Hopeful Valley.
You will say "Yes" to me
as you did in your youth,
   when leaving Egypt.
I promise that from that day on, you will
call me your husband instead of your
master. I will no longer even let you mention
the names of those pagan gods that you
called "Master." And I will agree to let you
live in peace—you will no longer be
attacked by wild animals and birds or by
weapons of war. I will accept you as my wife
forever, and instead of a bride price I will
give you justice, fairness, love, kindness,
and faithfulness. Then you will truly know
who I am.   HOSEA 2.13-20

I am the LORD your God.
   And you will know I live on Zion,
   my sacred hill,
because Jerusalem will be sacred,
   untouched by foreign troops.

On that day, fruitful vineyards
will cover the mountains.
And your cattle and goats
that graze on the hills
    will produce a lot of milk.
Streams in Judah will never run dry;
    a stream from my house
    will flow in Acacia Valley.

Egypt and Edom
were cruel and brutal to Judah,
    without a reason.
Now their countries
will become a barren desert,
    but Judah and Jerusalem
    will always have people.
I, the LORD, live on Mount Zion.
    I will punish the guilty
    and defend the innocent.   JOEL 3.17-21

My friends, I don't want you Gentiles to
be too proud of yourselves. So I will explain
the mystery of what has happened to the
people of Israel. Some of them have become
stubborn, and they will stay like that until
the complete number of you Gentiles has
come in. In this way all of Israel will be
saved, as the Scriptures say,

"From Zion someone will come
to rescue us.
Then Jacob's descendants
will stop being evil.
This is what the Lord
has promised to do
when he forgives their sins."

ROMANS 11.25–27

Return of Christ

ᘒ Soon you will see the Son of Man
sitting at the right side of God All-Powerful,
and coming with the clouds of heaven.

MARK 14.62

Look! He is coming with the clouds.
Everyone will see him,
even the ones who stuck
a sword through him.
All people on earth
will weep because of him.
Yes, it will happen! Amen. REVELATION 1.7

He will take his stand on the Mount of
Olives east of Jerusalem, and the mountain

will split in half, forming a wide valley that runs from east to west. Then you people will escape from the LORD's mountain, through this valley, which reaches to Azal. You will run in all directions, just as everyone did when the earthquake struck in the time of King Uzziah of Judah. Afterwards, the LORD my God will appear with his holy angels.   ZECHARIAH 14.4–5

With a loud command and with the shout of the chief angel and a blast of God's trumpet, the Lord will return from heaven. Then those who had faith in Christ before they died will be raised to life.

1 THESSALONIANS 4.16

So Christ died only once to take away the sins of many people. But when he comes again, it will not be to take away sin. He will come to save everyone who is waiting for him.   HEBREWS 9.28

The Lord meant that when you eat this bread and drink from this cup, you tell about his death until he comes.

1 CORINTHIANS 11.26

147

The Lord is my judge. So don't judge anyone until the Lord returns. He will show what is hidden in the dark and what is in everyone's heart. Then God will be the one who praises each of us.

1 CORINTHIANS 4.4-5

All of this shows that God judges fairly and that he is making you fit to share in his kingdom for which you are suffering. It is only right for God to punish everyone who is causing you trouble, but he will give you relief from your troubles. He will do the same for us, when the Lord Jesus comes from heaven with his powerful angels and with a flaming fire.   2 THESSALONIANS 1.5-8

Think how much the Father loves us. He loves us so much that he lets us be called his children, as we truly are. But since the people of this world did not know who Christ is, they don't know who we are. My dear friends, we are already God's children, though what we will be hasn't yet been seen. But we do know that when Christ returns, we will be like him, because we will see him as he truly is.   1 JOHN 3.1-2

I am coming soon! And when I come,
I will reward everyone for what they have
done. I am Alpha and Omega, the first and
the last, the beginning and the end.

REVELATION 22.12–13

Increase of Knowledge and Light

❧ You won't need the light
of the sun or the moon.
I, the LORD your God,
will be your eternal light
    and bring you honor.
Your sun will never set
or your moon go down.
I, the LORD, will be your everlasting light,
    and your days of sorrow
    will come to an end.
Your people will live right
and always own the land;
    they are the trees I planted
    to bring praise to me.

ISAIAH 60.19–21

I did not see a temple there. The Lord God All-Powerful and the Lamb were its temple. And the city did not need the sun or the moon. The glory of God was shining on it, and the Lamb was its light.

Nations will walk by the light of that city, and kings will bring their riches there. Its gates are always open during the day, and night never comes. The glorious treasures of nations will be brought into the city. But nothing unworthy will be allowed to enter. No one who is dirty-minded or who tells lies will be there. Only those whose names are written in the Lamb's book of life will be in the city. REVELATION 21.22–27

Just as water fills the sea,
the land will be filled
    with people who know
    and honor the LORD. HABAKKUK 2.14

The blind will see,
and the ears of the deaf will be healed.
Those who were lame will leap like deer;
    tongues once silent will begin to shout.
    Water will rush through the desert.

Scorching sand will turn into a lake,
    and thirsty ground
    will flow with fountains.
Grass will grow in wetlands,
where packs of wild dogs
    once made their home.
A good road will be there,
    and it will be named
    "God's Sacred Highway."
It will be for God's people;
no one unfit to worship God
    will walk on that road.
And no fools can travel on that highway.

ISAIAH 35.5–8

I will teach your children
and make them successful.   ISAIAH 54.13

The deaf will be able to hear
whatever is read to them;
    the blind will be freed
    from a life of darkness.
The poor and the needy
will celebrate and shout
    because of the LORD,
    the holy God of Israel.

ISAIAH 29.18–19

151

In the beginning was the one
who is called the Word.
The Word was with God and was truly God.
From the very beginning
the Word was with God.

And with this Word, God created all things.
Nothing was made without the Word.
Everything that was created
received its life from him,
and his life gave light to everyone.
The light keeps shining in the dark,
and darkness has never put it out.
God sent a man named John,
who came to tell about the light
and to lead all people to have faith.
John wasn't that light.
He came only to tell about the light.

The true light that shines on everyone
was coming into the world.
The Word was in the world,
but no one knew him,
though God had made the world
with his Word.
He came into his own world,
but his own nation did not welcome him.

Yet some people accepted him
and put their faith in him.
    So he gave them the right
    to be the children of God.
They were not God's children by nature
    or because of any human desires.
God himself was the one
who made them his children.

The Word became a human being
and lived here with us.
We saw his true glory,
    the glory of the only Son of the Father.
From him all the kindness
and all the truth of God
    have come down to us.   JOHN 1.1–14

Once again Jesus spoke to the people.
This time he said, "I am the light for the
world! Follow me, and you won't be walking
in the dark. You will have the light that
gives life."   JOHN 8.12

My dear friends, I am not writing to give
you a new commandment. It is the same
one that you were first given, and it is the
message you heard. But it really is a new
commandment, and you know its true

153

meaning, just as Christ does. You can see the darkness fading away and the true light already shining.

If we claim to be in the light and hate someone, we are still in the dark. But if we love others, we are in the light, and we don't cause problems for them. If we hate others, we are living and walking in the dark. We don't know where we are going, because we can't see in the dark.   1 JOHN 2.7-11

Final Peace

🕊 Please help the king
to be honest and fair
    just like you, our God.
Let him be honest and fair
with all your people,
    especially the poor.
Let peace and justice rule
every mountain and hill.   PSALM 72.1-3

Celebrate and be glad forever!
    I am creating a Jerusalem,
    full of happy people.

I will celebrate with Jerusalem
and all of its people;

> there will be no more crying or sorrow
> in that city. ISAIAH 65.18-19

Then the LORD will cover the whole city
and its meeting places with a thick cloud
each day and with a flaming fire each
night. God's own glory will be like a huge
tent that covers everything. It will provide
shade from the heat of the sun and a place
of shelter and protection from storms and
rain. ISAIAH 4.5-6

The LORD will teach us his Law
from Jerusalem,

> and we will obey him.

He will settle arguments between nations.
They will pound
their swords and their spears

> into rakes and shovels;

they will never make war
or attack one another. ISAIAH 2.3-4

Leopards will lie down with young goats,

> and wolves will rest with lambs.

Calves and lions will eat together

> and be cared for by little children.

Cows and bears
will share the same pasture;
their young will rest side by side.
    Lions and oxen will both eat straw.

ISAIAH 11.6–7

End of Evil

Our people defeated Satan
because of the blood of the Lamb
    and the message of God.

REVELATION 12.11

    Then God, who gives peace, will soon
crush Satan under your feet. I pray that our
Lord Jesus will be kind to you.

ROMANS 16.20

The Lord said to my Lord,
"Sit at my right side,
    until I make your enemies
    into a footstool for you."

The Lord will let your power
reach out from Zion,
    and you will rule over your enemies.

PSALM 110.1–2

The poor and the needy
will be treated with fairness
    and with justice.
His word will be law everywhere in the land,
    and criminals will be put to death.
Honesty and fairness will be his royal robes.

ISAIAH 11.4–5

Finally, let the mighty strength of the
Lord make you strong. Put on all the armor
that God gives, so you can defend yourself
against the devil's tricks. We are not
fighting against humans. We are fighting
against forces and authorities and against
rulers of darkness and powers in the
spiritual world. So put on all the armor that
God gives. Then when that evil day comes,
you will be able to defend yourself. And
when the battle is over, you will still be
standing firm.   EPHESIANS 6.10–13

When the seventy-two followers returned,
they were excited and said, "Lord, even the
demons obeyed when we spoke in your
name!"
    Jesus told them:
        I saw Satan fall from heaven like a
    flash of lightning. I have given you the

157

power to trample on snakes and
scorpions and to defeat the power of
your enemy Satan. Nothing can harm
you. But don't be happy because evil
spirits obey you. Be happy that your
names are written in heaven!

LUKE 10.17-20

"Deep in her heart Babylon said,
'I am the queen!
Never will I be a widow
    or know what it means to be sad.'
And so, in a single day
she will suffer the pain
    of sorrow, hunger, and death.
Fire will destroy her dead body,
    because her judge
    is the powerful Lord God."

REVELATION 18.7-8

Surrender to God! Resist the devil, and
he will run from you. Come near to God,
and he will come near to you. Clean up
your lives, you sinners. JAMES 4.7-8

I pray that you will be grateful to God
for letting you have part in what he has

promised his people in the kingdom of light. God rescued us from the dark power of Satan and brought us into the kingdom of his dear Son, who forgives our sins and sets us free.   COLOSSIANS 1.12–14

Anyone who keeps on sinning belongs to the devil. He has sinned from the beginning, but the Son of God came to destroy all that he has done. God's children cannot keep on being sinful. His life-giving power lives in them and makes them his children, so that they cannot keep on sinning. You can tell God's children from the devil's children, because those who belong to the devil refuse to do right or to love each other.   1 JOHN 3.8–10

Be on your guard and stay awake. Your enemy, the devil, is like a roaring lion, sneaking around to find someone to attack. But you must resist the devil and stay strong in your faith. You know that all over the world the Lord's followers are suffering just as you are.   1 PETER 5.8–9

Raised from the Dead

❧ I am your chosen one.
You won't leave me in the grave
    or let my body decay.
You have shown me the path to life,
    and you make me glad
    by being near to me.
Sitting at your right side,
I will always be joyful.   PSALM 16.10-11

Just as we will die because of Adam,
we will be raised to life because of Christ.
Adam brought death to all of us, and Christ
will bring life to all of us. But we must each
wait our turn. Christ was the first to be
raised to life, and his people will be raised
to life when he returns. Then after Christ
has destroyed all powers and forces, the
end will come, and he will give the kingdom
to God the Father.   1 CORINTHIANS 15.21-24

That's how it will be when our bodies are
raised to life. These bodies will die, but the
bodies that are raised will live forever. These
ugly and weak bodies will become beautiful

and strong. As surely as there are physical bodies, there are spiritual bodies. And our physical bodies will be changed into spiritual bodies. 1 CORINTHIANS 15.42–44

Everyone on earth has a body like the body of the one who was made from the dust of the earth. And everyone in heaven has a body like the body of the one who came from heaven. Just as we are like the one who was made out of earth, we will be like the one who came from heaven.

1 CORINTHIANS 15.48–49

I wish that my words could be written down
    or chiseled into rock.
I know that my Savior lives,
    and at the end
    he will stand on this earth.
My flesh may be destroyed,
    yet from this body I will see God.
Yes, I will see him for myself,
    and I long for that moment.

JOB 19.23–27

Yet God raised Jesus to life! God's Spirit now lives in you, and he will raise you to life by his Spirit. ROMANS 8.11

With a loud command and with the shout of the chief angel and a blast of God's trumpet, the Lord will return from heaven. Then those who had faith in Christ before they died will be raised to life.

1 THESSALONIANS 4.16

Don't be surprised! The time will come when all of the dead will hear the voice of the Son of Man, and they will come out of their graves. Everyone who has done good things will rise to life, but everyone who has done evil things will rise and be condemned. JOHN 5.28-29

Our Lord Jesus Christ has power over everything, and he will make these poor bodies of ours like his own glorious body.

PHILIPPIANS 3.20-21

Jesus then said, "I am the one who raises the dead to life! Everyone who has faith in me will live, even if they die. And everyone who lives because of faith in me will never really die." JOHN 11.25

Eternal Life

❧ God loved the people of this world so much that he gave his only Son, so that everyone who has faith in him will have eternal life and never really die.

JOHN 3.16

Now you have been set free from sin, and you are God's slaves. This will make you holy and will lead you to eternal life.

ROMANS 6.22

But no one who drinks the water I give will ever be thirsty again. The water I give is like a flowing fountain that gives eternal life.   JOHN 4.14

God has also said that he gave us eternal life and that this life comes to us from his Son. And so, if we have God's Son, we have this life.   1 JOHN 5.11–12

But the bread from heaven has come down, so that no one who eats it will ever die. I am that bread from heaven! Everyone who eats it will live forever. My flesh is the life-giving bread that I give to the people of this world.   JOHN 6.50-51

The Son has promised us eternal life.
1 JOHN 2.25

Jesus treated us much better
than we deserved.
He made us acceptable to God
and gave us the hope of eternal life.
TITUS 3.7

Everlasting Blessings

❧ So I will give you the right to rule as kings, just as my Father has given me the right to rule as a king. You will eat and drink with me in my kingdom, and you will each sit on a throne to judge the twelve tribes of Israel.   LUKE 22.29-30

Don't store up treasures on earth! Moths and rust can destroy them, and thieves can break in and steal them. Instead, store up your treasures in heaven, where moths and rust cannot destroy them, and thieves

cannot break in and steal them. Your heart
will always be where your treasure is.

MATTHEW 6.19–21

You won't need the light
of the sun or the moon.
I, the LORD your God,
will be your eternal light
    and bring you honor.
Your sun will never set
or your moon go down.
I, the LORD, will be your everlasting light,
    and your days of sorrow
    will come to an end.
Your people will live right
and always own the land;
    they are the trees I planted
    to bring praise to me.

ISAIAH 60.19–21

But it is just as the Scriptures say,
    "What God has planned
    for people who love him
    is more than eyes have seen
    or ears have heard.
      It has never even entered
      our minds!" 1 CORINTHIANS 2.9

"Wonderful!" his master replied. "You are a good and faithful servant. I left you in charge of only a little, but now I will put you in charge of much more. Come and share in my happiness!" MATTHEW 25.21

Praise God, the Father of our Lord Jesus Christ. God is so good, and by raising Jesus from death, he has given us new life and a hope that lives on. God has something stored up for you in heaven, where it will never decay or be ruined or disappear. 1 PETER 1.3-4

All who win the victory will be given these blessings. I will be their God, and they will be my people. REVELATION 21.7

My prayer is that light will flood your hearts and that you will understand the hope that was given to you when God chose you. Then you will discover the glorious blessings that will be yours together with all of God's people. EPHESIANS 1.18

Christ died to rescue those who had sinned and broken the old agreement. Now he brings his chosen ones a new

agreement with its guarantee of God's
eternal blessings! HEBREWS 9.15

There are many rooms in my Father's
house. I wouldn't tell you this, unless it was
true. I am going there to prepare a place for
each of you. After I have done this, I will
come back and take you with me. Then we
will be together. You know the way to where
I am going. JOHN 14.2-4

A Home with God

🐚 Our bodies are like tents that we live
in here on earth. But when these tents are
destroyed, we know that God will give each
of us a place to live. These homes will not
be buildings that someone has made, but
they are in heaven and will last forever.
While we are here on earth, we sigh
because we want to live in that heavenly
home. We want to put it on like clothes
and not be naked.

These tents we now live in are like a
heavy burden, and we groan. But we don't
do this just because we want to leave these

bodies that will die. It is because we want
to change them for bodies that will never
die. God is the one who makes all of this
possible. He has given us his Spirit to make
us certain that he will do it. So always be
cheerful!   2 CORINTHIANS 5.1-6

Then he said to Jesus, "Remember me
when you come into power!"
Jesus replied, "I promise that today you
will be with me in paradise."

LUKE 23.42-43

Your kindness and love
will always be with me
each day of my life,
    and I will live forever
    in your house, LORD.   PSALM 23.6

Then I saw New Jerusalem, that holy
city, coming down from God in heaven. It
was like a bride dressed in her wedding
gown and ready to meet her husband.

REVELATION 21.2

Because Abraham had faith, he lived as
a stranger in the promised land. He lived

there in a tent, and so did Isaac and Jacob,
who were later given the same promise.
Abraham did this, because he was waiting
for the eternal city that God had planned
and built.   HEBREWS 11.9-10

There are many rooms in my Father's
house. I wouldn't tell you this, unless it was
true. I am going there to prepare a place for
each of you. After I have done this, I will
come back and take you with me. Then we
will be together. You know the way to where
I am going.   JOHN 14.2-4

Unending Happiness

🐦 I am your chosen one.
You won't leave me in the grave
    or let my body decay.
You have shown me the path to life,
    and you make me glad
    by being near to me.
Sitting at your right side,
I will always be joyful.   PSALM 16.10-11

You won't need the light
of the sun or the moon.
I, the LORD your God,
will be your eternal light
    and bring you honor.
Your sun will never set
or your moon go down.
I, the LORD, will be your everlasting light,
    and your days of sorrow
    will come to an end.
Your people will live right
and always own the land;
    they are the trees I planted
    to bring praise to me.   ISAIAH 60.19–21

And so they stand before the throne of God
    and worship him in his temple
    day and night.
The one who sits on the throne
    will spread his tent over them.
They will never hunger or thirst again,
and they won't be troubled
    by the sun or any scorching heat.
                 REVELATION 7.15–16

All who win the victory will be given
these blessings. I will be their God,
and they will be my people.

REVELATION 21.7

I did not see a temple there. The Lord
God All-Powerful and the Lamb were its
temple. And the city did not need the sun or
the moon. The glory of God was shining on
it, and the Lamb was its light.

Nations will walk by the light of that city,
and kings will bring their riches there. Its
gates are always open during the day, and
night never comes. The glorious treasures
of nations will be brought into the city. But
nothing unworthy will be allowed to enter.
No one who is dirty-minded or who tells lies
will be there. Only those whose names are
written in the Lamb's book of life will be in
the city.   REVELATION 21.22-27

But God has promised us a Sabbath
when we will rest, even though it has not
yet come. On that day God's people will rest
from their work, just as God rested from his
work.   HEBREWS 4.9-10

All of this shows that God judges fairly and that he is making you fit to share in his kingdom for which you are suffering. It is only right for God to punish everyone who is causing you trouble, but he will give you relief from your troubles. He will do the same for us, when the Lord Jesus comes from heaven with his powerful angels and with a flaming fire.   2 THESSALONIANS 1.5-8

But it is just as the Scriptures say,
"What God has planned
for people who love him
is more than eyes have seen
or ears have heard.
It has never even entered
our minds!"   1 CORINTHIANS 2.9

Glory Forever

Holy, holy, holy, LORD All-Powerful!
The earth is filled with your glory.

ISAIAH 6.3

172

Celebrate and be glad forever!
　　I am creating a Jerusalem,
　　full of happy people.
I will celebrate with Jerusalem
and all of its people;
　　there will be no more crying or sorrow
　　in that city.　ISAIAH 65.18–19

　　Our Lord Jesus Christ has power over
everything, and he will make these poor
bodies of ours like his own glorious body.
　　　　　　　　　　　　PHILIPPIANS 3.20–21

Open the ancient gates,
　　so that the glorious king may come in.

Who is this glorious king?
　　He is our LORD,
　　a strong and mighty warrior.

Open the ancient gates,
　　so that the glorious king may come in.

Who is this glorious king?
　　He is our LORD, the All-Powerful!
　　　　　　　　　　　PSALM 24.7–10

Your great victory will be seen
by every nation and king;
    the LORD will even give you a new name.
You will be a glorious crown,
a royal headband,
    for the LORD your God. ISAIAH 62.2-3

God's Spirit makes us sure that we are
his children. His Spirit lets us know that
together with Christ we will be given what
God has promised. We will also share in the
glory of Christ, because we have suffered
with him.

I am sure that what we are suffering now
cannot compare with the glory that will be
shown to us. ROMANS 8.16-18

But everyone who has done right will
shine like the sun in their Father's kingdom.
                MATTHEW 13.43

Everyone who has been wise will shine
as bright as the sky above, and everyone
who has led others to please God will shine
like the stars. DANIEL 12.3

Christ gives meaning to your life, and when he appears, you will also appear with him in glory.   COLOSSIANS 3.4

He will give eternal life to everyone who has patiently done what is good in the hope of receiving glory, honor, and life that lasts forever.   ROMANS 2.7

Plan of Salvation

• You Are a Sinner . . .
   The Scriptures tell us,
      "No one is acceptable to God!"
                                             ROMANS 3.10

• There Is a Price to Be Paid for Sin . . .
   All of us have sinned and fallen short of God's glory.   ROMANS 3.23

• Need to Repent . . .
   Go and learn what the Scriptures mean when they say, "Instead of offering sacrifices to me, I want you to be merciful to others." I didn't come to invite good

people to be my followers. I came to invite
sinners.   MATTHEW 9.13

Not at all! But you can be sure that if
you don't turn back to God, every one of
you will also be killed.   LUKE 13.3

• God Loves You . . .
God loved the people of this world so
much that he gave his only Son, so that
everyone who has faith in him will have
eternal life and never really die.

JOHN 3.16

• Christ Died for You and Wants to Save
You . . .
Sin pays off with death. But God's gift is
eternal life given by Jesus Christ our Lord.

ROMANS 6.23

But God showed how much he loved us
by having Christ die for us, even though we
were sinful.   ROMANS 5.8

• Christ Will Save You Now . . .
So you will be saved, if you honestly say,
"Jesus is Lord," and if you believe with all
your heart that God raised him from death.

God will accept you and save you, if you truly believe this and tell it to others.

ROMANS 10.9–10

All who call out to the Lord will be saved. ROMANS 10.13

• You Can Know That You Are Saved . . .

If we have faith in God's Son, we have believed what God has said. But if we don't believe what God has said about his Son, it is the same as calling God a liar. God has also said that he gave us eternal life and that this life comes to us from his Son. And so, if we have God's Son, we have this life. But if we don't have the Son, we don't have this life.

All of you have faith in the Son of God, and I have written to let you know that you have eternal life. We are certain that God will hear our prayers when we ask for what pleases him. And if we know that God listens when we pray, we are sure that our prayers have already been answered.

1 JOHN 5.10–15

The publisher hopes *Promises For Life* is a source of encouragement and spiritual uplift for you. Equally heartening is *The Promise*™, a Bible packed with the great promises God has made to his people. *The Promise*™ contains the complete text of the Contemporary English Version (CEV), plus 200 articles highlighting God's work in people's lives and in the world. Available at bookstores in these styles:

Full-color paperback   Style 3490   ISBN 0-8407-0459-3
Full-color hardcover   Style 3492   ISBN 0-8407-0460-7
Bonded leather   Style 3495   ISBN 0-8407-1849-7